The FAITH of
CONDOLEEZZA RICE

The FAITH *of*

CONDOLEEZZA RICE

LESLIE MONTGOMERY

CROSSWAY BOOKS

A PUBLISHING MINISTRY OF
GOOD NEWS PUBLISHERS
WHEATON, ILLINOIS

Cover design: Josh Dennis

Cover photo: Associated Press

First printing, 2007

Printed in the United States of America

Unless otherwise indicated, Scripture quotations are taken from *The Holy Bible: English Standard Version*®. Copyright © 2001 by Crossway Bibles, a publishing ministry of Good News Publishers. Used by permission. All rights reserved.

Library of Congress Cataloging-in-Publication Data

Montgomery, Leslie, 1967–
    The faith of Condoleezza Rice / Leslie Montgomery.
       p. cm.
    ISBN 13: 978-1-58134-799-9 (hc : alk. paper)
    ISBN 10: 1-58134-799-5
    1. Rice, Condoleezza, 1954–   . 2. Rice, Condoleezza, 1954–Religion.
3. Stateswomen–United States–Biography. 4. Women cabinet officers–
United States–Biography. 5. Cabinet officers–United States–Biography.
6. National Security Council (U.S.)–Biography. 7. African American
women–Biography. 8. African Americans–Biography I. Title.
E840.8.R48M66   2007
355'.033073092–dc22   2006033151

LB		17	16	15	14	13	12	11	10	09	08	07
15	14	13	12	11	10	9	8	7	6	5	4	3	2	1

Contents

IN THE GARDEN

I come to the garden alone,
While the dew is still on the roses;
And the voice I hear, falling on my ear,
The Son of God discloses.
And He walks with me,
And He talks with me,
And He tells me I am His own;
And the joy we share as we tarry there
None other has ever known.

He speaks, and the sound of His voice
Is so sweet that the birds hush their singing;
And the melody that He gave to me
Within my heart is ringing.
And He walks with me,
And He talks with me,
And He tells me I am His own;
And the joy we share as we tarry there
None other has ever known.

A favorite hymn of Condoleezza Rice, and a song that she and her father sang together frequently in the last days of his life.

Thank-yous

*W*ow! What an incredible project the writing of this book has been. There is no way I could have completed this book without the following people:

My Crossway crew who are not only my publisher, but co-laborers, friends, and prayer partners in this collaboration. *All* the staff at Crossway are a part of the finality and success of this book, and I am eternally grateful for your work and commitment on behalf of our God and King. I couldn't have done this without you.

All of Condoleezza's friends and family who so graciously allowed me to pry into their personal lives, ask intruding and sometimes stupid questions, and drag up the past. Writers are such pests, huh? Seriously though, every one of you made my job easier with your love of Condi, your faith in Jesus, and your support of this project.

Special thanks to Clara Bailey-Rice for sharing her family album, support, and encouragement and for allowing our long interview to flow over into a wonderful church service and the breaking of bread. You were really a blessing to me in so many ways. Let me know when you're ready to write that book we talked about!

Thanks to Susan Ford, John Leslie Blackburn, Moses Brewer, Lori White (you're great!), John Raisian, Holly Blackburn, Fred Shuttlesworth, Jackie Glaster, Annye Marie Downing, Mattie Ray-

Bond, and others who asked to remain anonymous for privacy reasons—you know who you are.

Thanks to Stanford University, Denver University, and the archive departments in the Birmingham and Denver Libraries for so graciously compiling pictures and research for this book. Your assistance was priceless.

Thanks to the staff at the Birmingham Civil Rights Museum and members of the 16th Street Baptist Church and Westminster Presbyterian Church for their tours, assistance, warmth, and encouragement during this project.

Thanks to Casting Crowns for feeding my soul during the writing of this book. I appreciate the fact that you're so bold and refuse to sell out for money and your own glory.

My husband Dallas, for holding me and encouraging me *every time* I cried on your shoulder during the frequent frustrating moments, for being my prayer covering, but most of all for being a godly man through and through. I love you, baby. You're my hero!

To my dad, Arthur B. Montgomery. Who would have ever thought I'd be writing books for a living the day you adopted me? Your love, support, and encouragement since has been the wind beneath my wings. Thanks for believing in me when no one else did.

Above all, for my Lord and King. You graciously allowed me to write this book and went ahead of me and prepared the miraculous way. Forgive me for my lack of faith. As usual, you exceeded all my expectations.

INTRODUCTION

*W*hen I first got the idea to write this book, I thought that any publisher would jump at the chance of printing a faith-based biography on Condoleezza Rice. Unfortunately, that wasn't the case. After going through two publishers who said yes and then changed their mind, I began to get a bit discouraged. I knew the Lord put the writing of this book on my heart, but it didn't seem like it was going to pan out. Then I started writing for Crossway, who saw working with me as a spiritual investment and collaboration on behalf of God's kingdom. They published two of my books back to back in 2006 and didn't hesitate when I asked them to consider this biography and the one to follow on the faith of Laura Bush. I was both encouraged and flabbergasted by their support.

I immediately began the research for this book, read every book I could find on Condoleezza Rice, compiled a list of names and phone numbers of people I'd like to interview, and put in a request to interview Condoleezza. The subsequent six-month wrestling match with the State Department public relations department ranged from "No, you can't have an interview" to "What day and time do you want to do it?" to "Dr. Rice doesn't have the time to meet with you due to the Middle East crisis." (Ah, the frustration that comes with not being Oprah or Tim Russert.) That emotional roller coaster ride caused a lot of unwanted (not to mention unneeded) frustration and anxiety. (Ironically, when the book was completed, Condi did get a copy from a family member, read it, and had her office call with changes she felt appropriate.)

Additionally, I must admit that as I did the extensive research necessary for this book, I often feared that I was in over my head. I'm not heavily educated in politics or its terms, but as I prayed, I felt strongly that the Lord was reminding me that this wasn't a book about politics but a book about faith. Although some would argue that the two often seem interchangeable, I heard what the Lord was saying, so I tried to stay true to my course.

You will find that I used the Civil Rights Movement as a guideline in this book. I did this because Condoleezza was raised during the most heated and turbulent years of the movement in the vortex of the most violent protests against segregation and liberation—Birmingham, Alabama. For those of you like me who were not raised in the South or educated in any extensive manner on the battle that ensued for and against freedom, I'm sure you will be as shocked as I was about the brutality of the perpetrators who sought to eliminate the black race at all costs and as impressed with the perseverance and righteous defiance of those who not only sought to survive it but thrive after it. Both the hunter and the hunted in the game of slavery and liberation are a part of Condoleezza's heritage, and both have helped develop her convictions and her faith, which have contributed to who she is today.

This book has been a labor of love, a challenge, and an education, heart-wrenching and yet encouraging, frustrating but satisfying. During the writing of it I often thought to myself, *This is the ninth book you've written. You're passionate about research and writing. Why is this project so hard?* In hindsight I see that it is because the Lord made me an emotional person, and the continual ups and downs of Condoleezza's family deeply affected me. At the same time, the determination of her forefathers to gain education and to stand against prejudice inspired me, her parents' spiritual convictions challenged me, her dedication and perseverance as a young child encouraged me, and the history of the blacks that went through hell on earth for the sake of liberation for their children and grandchildren hurt, angered, and motivated me.

Writing a book is often like putting a puzzle together. You have some idea of what the final product is supposed to look like, but as you look at some of the pieces you just can't figure out their purpose or place. Still, you grapple with the unknown, moving forward in faith, believing that at some point the unfamiliar parts will take form and start to look like that which you intended. Amazingly, the final product is always much more exquisite than the initial vision because as you wrestle with the unknown you become intimately familiar with it. Such is the case with this book. That which was vague and unclear now has a pristine clarity that rings true in my spirit. It is as if my vision was blurred at first but has suddenly become perfect. At the risk of sounding cliché, I was blind, but now I see—I see what God had in mind from the beginning. As a result I will remain forever changed by the completion of the picture this book paints and honored that the Lord chose me to paint it with words.

Ironically, the picture that unfolded for me during the writing of this book may not be the one that is revealed to you, the reader, for we all see people and life from a different perspective—one that is shaped by our own experiences, beliefs, hopes, and passions. So sit back and enjoy the unveiling of what I hope will be a life-changing experience for you as it was for me, and try to see the life and faith of Condoleezza Rice as told by her friends, family, and herself through me.

A STORY OF PREJUDICE AND PROMISE

$\mathcal{S}$he's been called the devil's handmaiden, a history-maker, a rock star, Bush's secret weapon, the most influential woman in the world, a rising star, a murderer due to the death toll in Iraq, and a race traitor among other things. Regardless of what opinion people come to about who she is or what label they've laid to rest on her character due to the often prejudiced and judgmental onslaught of the media or the difference of political views, everyone knows there's something uniquely different about the 5'7", African-American woman whom we currently refer to as our Secretary of State. She has a mysterious stability, an enigmatic air, and an inexplicable confidence that is void of pride—a trait that is hard to find in the world, let alone in the White House or politics. Condoleezza's impenetrable strength, mysterious ambience, and unshakable temperament are all evidence of three defining characteristics—a faith that runs deep in her heritage, a personal passion for God that runs thick through her veins, and moral convictions that are by-products of both.

To know and appreciate the faith of Condoleezza Rice, no matter what your religious preference, you must learn about hers. To understand her passion for peace, you must become personally familiar with the chaotic state of the nation in which she was born, and you must be willing to become intimate enough with her fervor for tranquillity that you risk becoming an advocate of it yourself. To fully grasp her heart and what has motivated and pushed her to break and far exceed the limited expectations that enslaved both her race and gender for hundreds of generations before her, you must examine her roots. To taste the inspiration for democracy that flows like a river from her heart, you must learn what it is that feeds her soul. This book reveals all of this and more.

This book is not about politics. It's about a little black girl who was born into a faith-based home in the center of the most racially explosive town of the Civil Rights Movement—Birmingham, Alabama. It's about two parents who defied discrimination, stood against injustice, clung to their faith, rose above all expectations, and raised their child to follow the Lord they themselves served. They believed wholeheartedly that she was a gift from God born for such a time as this and that he had a special plan and a purpose for her life—a plan for good, and not for evil, a plan to give her a hope and a future—all this despite what the world dictated to them through hatred and prejudice that hovered over them without a hint of mercy.

THE BIRTH OF A LEADER

Condoleezza was born at 11:30 A.M. on November 14, 1954, nine months to the day after her parents were married. According to her relatives, she was not given a middle name because "with a first name like Condoleezza, you don't need a middle one." Her name is a twist on an Italian musical term (*con dolcezza*) that instructs the musician to play softly or literally "with sweetness." It's a prophecy of sorts for those who know her best, whether she's playing the piano or intervening and advocating for peace in the Middle East.

The year of Condi's birth was a year of promise for the black race in the United States. It was the year that the Supreme Court declared "separate but equal" schools unconstitutional, assuring minorities that a change for the better was in the air. Black Americans had worked hard up to this point, diligently striving for democracy in a nation that was founded on the belief that all men were created equal but up to that point hadn't stood by its own words. Still, the strides that had been made for equal rights in the years that preceded Condoleezza's birth helped pave the way for the landmark case of *Brown v. Board of Education*, which integrated schools throughout America.

One of the most significant events in United States history that helped prepare the change for liberation occurred in 1831 when Nat Turner led black slaves in a revolt against the oppression of white slave owners. Thirty-two years later, in 1863, President Lincoln, a slave owner himself, issued the Emancipation Proclamation, freeing slaves. Three years later the Civil Rights Act provided every citizen, regardless of race, sex, or religious beliefs, with full rights and privileges of citizenship under the U.S. Constitution. As a result of these changes, an outpouring of black culture, literature, music, and drama infiltrated America with the surety that all things were possible for those who believed it to be so.

As a result of these foundational steps as well as multiple others that preceded and succeeded them, approximately six months before Condi was born, the Supreme Court ordered public schools to desegregate. The revolutionary case of *Brown v. Board of Education* overturned the separate-but-equal doctrine, which dated back to 1896. The day of the ruling became known as Black Monday.[1]

Although the fight against segregation gained strength for African-Americans, the harder blacks pushed for freedom, the more their adversaries pushed back in resistance, using violence to preserve their unjust desires for segregation. When Condi wasn't even a month old, twelve hundred white men gathered in Selma, Alabama to attend the first mass meeting of the newly organized White Citizens Council to protest school segregation. They vowed to do whatever it took to keep the black race separate from what they viewed as the superior white race.

Many blacks, empowered for the first time in hundreds of years by desegregation, began to strive for an education, to attain a profession outside of the plantation where they had been working for their white masters, and to have a family of their own to raise—not to give to their owners as their property to work the fields. White supremacists continued to fight the liberation, further oppressing blacks, continuing to take what wasn't theirs, and using force and intimidation to keep blacks in bondage.

As a result, on both sides of her family Condi (as she prefers to be called) is descended from white slave owners who preyed on immoral and illegal sexual "rights" to their black slaves. Although it was not unusual in that day and time for slave owners to rape or engage in sexual relations with their slave women, the frequent brutality of the act further enslaved, intimidated, and bred inferiority.

In Condi's black heritage, the slaves were mostly house slaves rather than field slaves, and while this gave her great- and great-great-grandparents proximity to privilege, including some education, it was under the iron clasp of oppression and slavery that they attained or used it.

Most black slaves were given the opportunity to attend their church of faith on the Sabbath, which quickly became an educational warehouse for many where they learned to read, write, and expand their knowledge of their Constitutional and God-given rights as Americans and human beings in general. The more they learned, the more they realized that white men had the upper hand as long as they stayed ignorant of their rights, unable to read and write, and excluded from attaining a good profession and saving money. In short, their lack of education and knowledge kept them in bondage to the white man. So blacks' goals quickly became to get as educated as they could and to prepare their children from birth to do the same.

The newfound "freedom" that blacks were experiencing stimulated them to want to get high school diplomas and attend college, and as a result many black colleges were founded. What they didn't know was that while laws were being passed allotting them freedom, they would have to literally rip their liberation away from white-knuckled racists who would adamantly resist their attaining it. Hindsight reveals that America was talking out of both sides of her mouth. On one side she proclaimed, "We the people," offering equal rights; but on the other side she demanded "separate but equal," an oxymoron at best. The contradiction was passionately challenged by blacks—either the Constitution was for every man, woman, and child, regardless of race or gender, or not for anyone. For Condoleezza and her family, this is where blatant defiance and confrontation against the system began—with two men she refers to as her heroes—her grandfathers.

A History of Education

The unspoken attitude among black family members seemed to be that the battle against racism wasn't only about what whites were doing to blacks, but what they themselves were or weren't doing for themselves. Thus black parents and grandparents became motivated to do all they could do to educate their lineage in ways of which they themselves had remained in ignorance. As a result Condi's grandparents, specifically her grandfathers, worked diligently to prepare the way for her parents and, indirectly, her.

Condoleezza's Granddaddy Rice (as she calls him), John Wesley Rice, Sr., had been one of nine children born to house slaves in Eutah, Alabama, eighty-nine miles southwest of Birmingham. Unlike some of their relatives and friends, who had been field slaves who worked their master's crops from sunrise to sunset, sometimes for eighteen hours a day, they lived more comfortably and were sometimes given "benefits" such as the family's used clothing and a limited education.

Granddaddy Rice hated racism and the inferiority that it bred in the black race. A man of faith in the Methodist denomination, he knew it was not God's will or plan for blacks to be treated as inferior to any other race. He vowed to break free from the confines of racism and to help others do the same.

After leaving home as a young man, Granddaddy Rice became a sharecropper on his own land. He didn't make much money—barely enough to get by—but at least he was free, unlike his parents and grandparents before him. A burning desire within him longed for an education in biblical studies. For generations, under the strictest confines of slavery in the harshest conditions, his forefathers had relied on the promises in the Bible and the strength through adversity that came with the saving knowledge of Jesus Christ. Now he wanted to learn everything he could about God's Word so he could share the internal liberation that he himself experienced with other African-Americans who didn't know about the freedom found in Christ.

One day in 1918 he asked someone passing by where a colored man could go to school to get "book learning." He was informed that there was a small Presbyterian school about thirty-seven miles north of Eutah in Tuscaloosa, Alabama, called Stillman College. It was a small, white-run seminary that specifically trained black men as Presbyterian ministers. So the elder Rice began to persevere and save cotton from the fields that he toiled in every day so he could pay for his education. When he finally made it to Stillman and had finished his first year, he realized that he had no way to pay for the remainder of his schooling. He inquisitively asked how the other young men were paying for their education, and he was told that they had received scholarships that paid for all of their schooling by agreeing to be trained to be Presbyterian pastors. School administrators told him that if he wanted to become a Presbyterian minister, he too could have a scholarship. He agreed, assuring them that attaining biblical knowledge to share with others was exactly what he had intended on doing in the first place. He got his degree in 1920 and was sent to plant an African-American church in Birmingham called Westminster Presbyterian Church.

After the church was up and running, Granddaddy Rice made it a personal mission from God to help the parents in the church send their children to college, particularly Stillman College. According to Condi's family, every year until his death he traveled to the Stillman campus by bus (he never owned a car) to advocate for students whose unpaid tuition bills otherwise would have disqualified them from taking finals and graduating. And every year students who would not have otherwise taken their finals because of a lack of finances did so with his intervention. Unfortunately, although Condi would learn to understand how her grandfather helped prepare the way for her own education, she never got to know him personally. He died two years before she was born.

"What my grandfather understood, and what I experienced years later, is the transforming power of education. And just as education transforms individuals, one by one, it can transform whole societies. Education is, as the American philosopher John Dewey believed, 'the fundamental method of social progress and reform.'"[2]

Condi's Granddaddy Rice was known for his passion for two things—education and Jesus Christ, both of which had liberated him. His picture hangs neatly in the midsized church today, and members say he was known for walking throughout the neighborhood personally inviting people to attend his church and share in the joy of salvation. He was a people person and spent hours visiting and encouraging his congregation. He saw it as his mission to evangelize as he emphasized freedom through Christ and education to anyone with a listening ear.

Condi's maternal grandfather, Albert Robinson Ray III or "Granddaddy Ray" as she prefers, was equally as impressive in his determination and perseverance. He was the son of a white plantation owner and a favored black servant from an educated family. Two maternal aunts were among the first nursing graduates from Tuskegee Medical Institute, founded by Booker T. Washington, who had a vision similar to that of Condi's ancestors—progress through education, self-reliance, and patience.[3]

In rebellion against segregation and degradation, Albert Ray ran away from home when he was thirteen years old with nothing but a railroad token in his pocket. He later married and had five children, settling down in Birmingham. At that time Birmingham was referred to as the Promised City for blacks, as it was the back-breaking labor of blacks that had fueled the progress and growth of the city when it originated in 1870. While other black kids were being raised to work for white families in order to financially assist their own families, Albert's children were forbidden to do so. He refused to allow the segregation to affect his family and stood against it in every way possible, including not allowing his children to drink from "colored" fountains or to use "colored" restrooms. Instead he encouraged his children to wait and use the facilities at home—or not at all. To succumb to using "colored" accommodations or to sit at the back of the bus was to submit to inferiority, and that was something the Rays just didn't do.

Angelena's brother Alto says he never got on a segregated bus in his life. "Daddy told us, 'Wait till you get home to drink. Wait till you get home to go to the bathroom.' If you had to go in the back door, we just wouldn't go."[4]

To properly care for his family, Granddaddy Ray worked two jobs during the week as a mining contractor and a blacksmith, and on Saturdays he built houses for extra money in the most segregated part of Birmingham. He was determined that his children would never work in the mines like he did. He had a reputation for two things—doing good work and not working on the Sabbath.

On Sundays Granddaddy Ray and his family spent the greater part of the day praising God and thanking him for their blessed life. In the African Methodist Episcopal Church, Granddaddy Ray was a trustee, a job he took seriously. Not only was he active in the church, but he was the spiritual leader of his family, a role that was even more important to him. As a family, the Rays prayed and read the Bible together on a daily basis. Again and again he told his children that segregation and racism was not about them but about man's desire to control and limit another person. It was an issue that had been around from the beginning of time, something the Bible itself advocated against. He also told them not to submit to the confines of intolerance in any way. It was not the Ray thing to do, or God's desire for his children.

Apart from faith in God, he also had a passion for education, seeing the collaboration of the two as a way to further liberate his children and future grandchildren. As a result he and his wife worked hard to put all five of their children through college. Eventually, as they grew into adults, he built homes for his children.

"I think that black Americans of my grandparents' ilk had liberated themselves," Condi says. "They had broken the code. They had figured out how to make an extraordinary comfortable and fulfilling life despite the circumstances. They did not feel that they were captives."[5] She also says, "One of my favorite quotes from Thomas Jefferson is: 'The God who gave us life gave us liberty at the same time.'"

Although Condi refers to her grandfathers as two of her favorite heroes because of their ability to overcome circumstances, the character traits of ambition and perseverance are part of her heritage that expands beyond those men. Condi says that one family member, a slave, taught herself how to read, others scrimped money together to buy books to educate themselves, and another adamantly pursued parish ministry in the Methodist denomination. There was great pride and determination in both the Ray and Rice heritage. Condi recalls her Grandma Ray continually telling her and her cousins to never forget that they were Rays, a reminder to stand tall, be proud, and demonstrate integrity in all they said and did.

Condi's maternal great-grandmother made a name for herself as well. Raised in Dolomite, a suburb in North Birmingham, Alabama, she was raised in the Colored Methodist Episcopal (CME) denomination, which changed to Christian Methodist Episcopal after integration and eventually became St. Paul's Christian Methodist Episcopal Chapel. She made a living by sewing for people and would often sew clothes for her granddaughters, one of which was Condi's mother, Angelena. Ang, as those who knew her best called her, and her older sister, Mattie, wearing their grandmother's hand-sewed dresses, would one day be used as models for a calendar, earning them the nickname Poster-Girls by friends in the community. Condi's great-grandmother's homemade dresses made their way into many homes, and some of Birmingham's elite sought her out for her sewing ability.

Interestingly enough, most of Condi's family members and forefathers were exceedingly successful in whatever they put their hand to. They were determined, hard-working, persevering, patient, and brimming with faith in God.

Aside from the contention that existed in the 1950s for black Americans to gain equal rights, another important movement and change was in effect—women's rights. Condoleezza's birth occurred during a decade of change for women. Despite the leaps and bounds occurring, women were still imprisoned by the tyranny of the government through unequal laws. The unrighteous, enslaving laws were even worse for black women. Without intervention some of those laws would not have enabled Condoleezza to go to college, vote, or retain a position in the upper echelons of government.

Although the movement by women to achieve full civil rights in America began in 1848 and had a good hundred years of success behind it by the time Condi was born, the residual effects of seven generations of beliefs that women were inferior to men continued to permeate the fifties and sixties. Although staggering changes were evident, there were areas of a woman's life that still needed to be liberated, specifically when it came to family life, religion, government, employment, and education. Regardless of the laws that had changed, within the hearts and minds of many people, predominantly males, there remained an attitude of superiority, and that was something laws couldn't change. As a result women would still have to fight to have equal wages in the workforce, be treated equally in regard to value, gain extended education, and overcome the inferiority that had been oppressing them their entire lives.

Given the cultural wars of racism and the ongoing battle for women's rights, it would have seemed implausible to imagine that a black, female child born in the heat of the battles at hand and the aftermath that has continued since would rise above the ruins to be a champion of sorts, not only for a nation but for a world. On January 25, 2005 United States Senator Joe Lieberman (Connecticut), in his statement on the nomination of Condoleezza Rice for Secretary of State, said:

> Let us speak directly. Dr. Rice, born in 1954 in the then racially segregated South, knew the sting of bigotry. No one on the day of her birth could have rationally predicted that she would grow up to be the Secretary of State of the United States of America. But she was blessed with great natural abilities, with a strong family, with an abiding faith in God.

God had prepared a life for Condoleezza Rice from the beginning of time and was orchestrating the dynamics of a universe to fulfill that calling. It included a plan that no one could overcome with bigotry, racism, or discrimination. He knew generations before she was born that her ancestors would fulfill their life plan and endure grave heartache and suffering in their attempt to pave the way of liberation, so she could fulfill his plans in her life. Her forefathers knew their hard work and determination would reap reward somewhere down the line, if not eternally. So they raised their children in liberty with the same recipe for success they had followed: faith, family, and education.

A LOVE STORY

The unwritten but not unspoken test among black Americans of how well their family functions is how well they care for their dependent members, particularly and most especially their children. In the early 1900s through the 1970s, children were the centerpiece of the African-American family, and often the foundation of their lives. For John and Angelena Rice, this was certainly the case, a passion each shared individually before joining in marriage and having their daughter.

John Wesley Rice, Jr., was born in Baton Rouge, Louisiana in 1923. His father was a Presbyterian minister and his mother a housewife. The baby of two children and the only boy, John was raised attending a segregated school, playing and excelling in sports.

After graduating from high school, he received a Bachelor of Arts and a Bachelor of Divinity from Johnson C. Smith University in Charlotte, North Carolina. He was a member of Phi Delta Kappa, an educational fraternity, and Alpha Phi Alpha, the first intercollegiate, black, Greek-letter fraternity, established by African-American students in 1906. Fresh out of college, John obtained a job as the director of the Petersburg Presbyterian Mission in Burlington, North Carolina.

A high school basketball and football player, he had a love for sports and a passion and dream for coaching. So when he was asked to be the director of physical education and a coach at Fairfield Industrial High School in Fairfield, Alabama, close to his family in Birmingham, it was an easy decision to make for the sports enthusiast.

John was a gifted coach, leading both his basketball and football teams to many victories, but it was really his mentoring that left the greatest impression on the young, moldable minds he taught. Everywhere John went, youth followed. He was known among the young men for being humorous, a good listener, and quite a storyteller. John encouraged the youth he mentored to ask questions, defend what they knew to be true, and question and stand against what society force-fed them in regard to their value as blacks.

Although John was fulfilling a part of him that loved sports, another aspect of the big, burly, deep-voiced man had yet to be utilized—his passion for God and his degree in divinity. He knew he wanted to mentor and teach young minds, but he wanted to do so with his faith as the driving rod that steered him. His father's example as a pastor had left him with a desire to preach the truth that he himself had been raised on. So in 1951 when John's father extended him a part-time position in Birmingham, Alabama as the religious education director for Westminster Presbyterian Church, he took the job. In accepting the position, he was able to retain his job at Fairfield Industrial High School.

John loved children and someday desired to marry and have an entire football team of boys. In the meantime, however, he'd have to settle for being a father figure to the black youth in Birmingham. Because the black youth were banned from public restaurants, pools, and Kiddieland, the local amusement park, he created a youth ministry at Westminster as an outreach and implemented a Youth Night to get the children in the community involved with something healthy and keep them out of trouble.

John's part-time work with the youth at Westminster Presbyterian

Church was so effective that young adults from other churches and communities poured into the building. John's popularity and reputation grew, causing quite a ruckus with other churches that were losing their youth to attend Westminster Youth Night. John boldly went into the housing projects to recruit underprivileged children to join them. Even some middle-class blacks balked at the idea of having "those" children there, but John was quick to tell them that they were all God's children and needed the encouragement and mentorship that their own children were being given. As a result of his persistence and love for the youth, he became a modern-day hero to black children in the Birmingham area.

"Rev," or "Daddy Rice" as the kids called him, made sure there were always fun and exciting things to do. He threw coed dances, Ping-Pong tournaments, field trips to various educational sites, board games, Bible studies, and afterschool sports activities. John's message to the kids he mentored and taught was the same he'd have for his own daughter when she was born. It came straight out of the Bible (Jeremiah 29:11-13): God has a plan for your life; a plan that is good and not for evil. It's a plan to give you a hope and a future.

John worked at Fairfield Industrial High School teaching physical education and coaching full-time and worked at the church in the evenings and on the weekends, although his involvement with young adults didn't stop there. He also served as a guidance counselor at the school and was active in a Drug Addiction Committee and was involved with other various programs. He jumped at any opportunity he was given to encourage and mentor black youth.

A little over two years later, John became the church's pastor when his father passed away. Westminster Presbyterian Church members adored John. Like his father, he was hands-on and made multiple personal visits and phone calls during the week to his congregation, praying and reading the Bible to those who could not do so on their own. His phone calls and check-ins with his congregation became such a big part of his life that he continued to do it throughout the rest of his life. He cared about people, and they knew it.

The year was 1952, and at the age of twenty-eight the then single pastor wanted to vote for the first time in his life. Unfortunately, the Democrats in Alabama would not register him to vote because he was black. When he attempted to do so anyway, he was given an "eligibility test" purposely orchestrated to keep anyone from passing. John's test consisted of a white clerk showing him a jar of jelly beans and asking how many were in it. When he failed to give the correct answer, he was denied registration. Other blacks were given equally absurd tests that they failed. It was a no-win situation reserved for any man or woman of color. The message was clear: blacks were not welcome to vote, and thus they would not be allotted the same rights and privileges as their white counterparts.

Although Democrats then controlled the registrars along with other offices, a woman at the courthouse would register blacks after-hours to help build the Republican Party. The plan succeeded, and hundreds of blacks, including John, became eligible to vote as Republicans as a result.

Angelena was born on July 23, 1924 and was the middle child in a family of five children—two boys and three girls. The Ray children lived with their parents in Dolomite, Alabama, a suburb in North Birmingham, in a home on 4th Street West that their father had built with his own hands. Although Angelena's mother could sew like her mother, her real love was teaching music, a gift she taught her children first and foremost, including Angelena. Angelena's grandmother was a pianist, and a good one at that, and taught Angelena's mother how to play. So when she had children, she passed on the legacy. In addition to adamantly teaching her children how to play the piano, she encouraged all five children to learn to play other instruments, making the Ray household quite musical—not to mention loud at times. Angelena's mother earned extra money for her household by teaching children and adults in Dolomite how to play piano. Added to her husband's income, this enabled them to buy a car, a rarity for blacks at that time.

"Anyone who knew how to play the piano in North Birmingham owed it to our mother," says Mattie Ray-Bond, Angelena's older sister. "We had a music room in our house, and that's where she taught piano. She was always at the piano, and always playing. She was the church organist and played at our school too."

Mattie and Ang, as those close to her called her, were as close as two sisters could be, spending as much of their time together as possible. They were less than a year and a half apart in age and had such a unique relationship that people called them the "Ray Twins." For fun, the two girls would practice and play duets on the piano. They both loved to play and perform for others, especially their parents. Their father's favorite song was an ode to heaven, "When They Ring the Golden Bells (For You and Me)," and the girls would practice it on the piano throughout the day and sing it for him in the evenings after he'd come home from a long day of providing for his family.

All of the Ray children learned to play music easily and quickly. "Everybody in the family was a natural when it came to playing music. We'd just hear anything and be able to play it," Mattie remembers. "We were specifically fond of playing hymns because we grew up in the church, but Ang had a more natural gift than any of us—Ang and our mother. We believed it was a gift from God."

Along with her brothers and sisters, Angelena attended school in the local church until a school building was built when she was in the sixth grade. Unlike today's academics, Scripture memorization was a part of learning and was mandatory. The black churches purposely sought to provide teachers who were not only capable of teaching academics but were also fluent in educating from the Bible, thus making sure their children were as well-versed in the Scriptures as they were in math or spelling.

Although blacks were segregated, Mattie says that the Ray children were often oblivious to it: "We were sheltered or guarded against it. I don't really know how except to say that we weren't encouraged that we were different, so we just lived life as if it [segregation] didn't exist. It was understood that we would accomplish that which whites did; we would succeed and go to college—there was no question or doubts about that in the Ray household." To combat the existing racism, the Ray children were encouraged by their parents to read everything they could get their hands on to further their knowledge, and not to succumb to the stereotyping by white America. As a matter of fact, their father would forbid them to use public facilities that were labeled "colored" and encouraged them not to frequent stores or restaurants that treated them as less than their white counterparts.

Segregation did not hold the Ray family down. Like many other black families, they built self-contained and self-sustained communities around them and purposely were not reliant on the white community in any way.

After high school, Angelena received her Bachelor of Arts from Miles College, graduating in 1945. She went on to teach English, art, and drama at Fairfield Industrial High School, where nine years later she met her future husband. As the story is told by family members, John walked into the teachers' lounge and was joking around with various teachers when he spotted the petite, shy, but beautiful woman he would eventually marry. He was immediately smitten and asked her out on a date, which ultimately led to several more.

Angelena's family loved John from the moment they met him. His zeal for life and love for Christ fit perfectly into their own spiritual beliefs and passion for God, and the fact that he was well-educated was the icing on the cake. Although the family belonged to the African Methodist Episcopal Church, upon meeting John they became Presbyterians, although not all officially joined the church. He immediately won the blessing from Angelena's parents to date and marry their daughter. He was, after all, a lot like her father—determined, focused, and extremely family-oriented.

John and Angelena, both in their thirties, married on Valentine's Day in 1954 and moved into the back of Westminster Presbyterian

Church where its members had built a small, four-room home for the pastor and his family. Within weeks of tying the knot, Angelena realized that she was pregnant. John was ecstatic and went out and bought what he hoped would be a boy his first football. He had a goal in mind for the baby growing in his wife's womb. He would name him after himself and coach him to be an All-American quarterback or linebacker who would attend and play for Notre Dame.

The church congregation was ecstatic for John and Angelena and their coming arrival. Many prayers of thanks to God were offered up, and Angelena was given a lot of support by other women in the church.

"I met Reverend Rice at my in-laws when I was visiting one summer," remembers Annye Marie Downing. "He'd stop by and talk and invite me to his church. My husband and I lived in Montgomery, but we eventually moved to Birmingham, and John gave us literature about Presbyterianism. I went to his church and met Ang. We were both pregnant—she with Condi and me with my first child.

"One of the things I loved about the Rices is that they lived their faith. Reverend Rice was never one to preach fire and brimstone to you. Instead, he lived his faith in the way he treated people and through his Scripture lessons. He loved children, and that was so Christ-like. Children followed him everywhere he went."

Fairfield Industrial High School had a rule that husband and wife could not work at the same location. So John transferred to the Birmingham School District across town, while Angelena continued to teach at Fairfield the rest of the school year, which was only a few months.

When the day came that Angelena went into labor, she and her newborn daughter were housed in the basement ward of the local hospital. Access to medical care in Birmingham was restricted based on race. Area hospitals housed black patients in segregated basement wards, and until 1954 not a single black doctor had hospital privileges since the county medical association accepted no black members. It would be another ten years before Holy Family Hospitals opened to serve black patients and doctors.

The day Condi was born and John saw that she was a girl, he determined that although she'd never be his quarterback for Notre Dame, he would teach her everything there was to know about football. So from day one if there was a football game on television, Condi was on his lap watching with her father. From as early as she remembers, her father gave her a detailed explanation of the game—the rules, regulations, and strategies. Condi fell in love with the game and the men who played it. "When I grow up I'm going to marry a professional football player!" Condi announced one day to a friend's mother.[1] As a matter of fact, she and her father watched all sports together—football, hockey, basketball, even sumo wrestling. John taught Condi to love competition. Condi was John's Little Star, a name he'd call her for the rest of his life.

John and Angelena took their role as parents very seriously. "Condi doesn't belong to us," John told numerous people. "She belongs to God."

Angelena took a year off from teaching to care for the newborn. After that initial year, Condi was left with Grandma Ray during the week while John and Angelena taught school.

John and Angelena were hands-on parents, and they took Condi everywhere they went when they weren't teaching. She was never left with a baby-sitter apart from her grandmother. Even when she was old enough to play with other children, she always did so within her mother's view. As a result of continual parental contact, Condi matured quickly and was exposed to a variety of adult activities such as opera, plays, and educational programs at an early age.

"Angelena's relationship with Condi is what I would call perfect," says her sister Mattie. "Condi was her entire world and seldom left her sight, and she never even talked about having another baby because she didn't want to share her love for Condi."

Annye Marie Downing echoes the same sentiment. "Angelena

would come to church with Condoleezza in both her hands like she was holding a little tray. She was devoted to her daughter and doted over her. Everything was for Condi—*everything*. I would take my kids to their home in the back of the church, and we'd sit on the floor and play with them. Condi only played indoors, so she was always around her mother and other adults.

"I once said to Angelena, 'You need another child,' and she said, 'No, I have to give all my love to Condi.' And whatever Condi did, her parents put all they had into it. When Ang and I were talking on the phone later in Condi's life and she said that Condi wanted to go study and learn Russian and take a year and spend it overseas, I said, 'Well, Ang, I know you'll be taking up stakes and going to Russia.' When Condi went to Notre Dame, I said, 'Are you and John moving over to Indiana?'

"Ang and I would joke a lot. I teased her about Condoleezza and all her love going to her, but she and John saw Condi as a gift from God and a treasure they were called to invest in. If there was ever a child who could have been spoiled rotten, it could have been Condoleezza, but she never showed a spoiled inch of herself. She was always friendly with other children in church and was just a sweet child. She was well-mannered and respectful in every area."

The new Rice family was very close from day one. Like Angelena, John sacrificially put their daughter above everything else in life. He was a good provider, and everyone in the church he pastored knew that his wife and daughter were his top priority.

"Reverend Rice put them before everything," remembers Downing. "Everything that he was called on to do, he did it only after he took care of Ang and Condoleezza. They were strong in their faith in God, reserved as a family, and devoted and loyal to one another."

Like many babies born into a faith-based home and specifically in the Presbyterian denomination, Condi was dedicated and baptized by her father at an early age in the Westminster Presbyterian Church. The family continued to live in the back of the church until the congregation contracted to have a modest parsonage on the corner of Center Way South West and Ninth Terrace in Birmingham built when Condi was barely two. The home was in a middle-class, predominantly black area of town just a few blocks from the church and would serve nicely for the years to come.

The same year Condi was born, Eugene "Bull" Connor became a candidate for the second time for governor of Alabama. Connor was known as a hard-line, outspoken Southern racist. Born in Selma, Alabama, Connor eventually ended up living in Birmingham in the late 1920s, serving as a radio broadcaster for the local minor league baseball team, the Birmingham Barons. In 1936 Connor was elected to the office of police commissioner, beginning the first of two stretches that spanned a total of twenty-three years. Connor's first tenure ended in 1952 but resumed in 1956 with a renewed passion and hatred toward black Americans—especially those who lived in his community. Birmingham voters—the majority of them white during this era of segregation—supported him and his bitter hatred toward blacks for many years.

Connor was so full of hatred that he swore to arrest any whites, or "commies" as he called them, if they talked to or advocated for blacks in any way. In May 1948, at Connor's orders, his officers arrested the U.S. Senator from Idaho, Glen H. Taylor, the running mate of progressive presidential candidate (and former Democratic Vice President) Henry Wallace. Taylor, who had attempted to speak to the Southern Negro Youth Congress, was arrested for violating Birmingham's segregation laws. During the Democratic National Convention that year Connor led the Alabama delegation in a walk-out when the party included a civil rights plank in its platform.

After becoming a candidate for governor of Alabama, Connor announced he would, among other things, be campaigning on the platform of segregation. Connor was not elected governor but instead remained the police commissioner and became notorious for his attacks against African-American demonstrators and civil rights leaders. He gained lasting infamy when he resorted to using water hoses and police dogs against protestors.

"I was in the heat of political struggle all through my childhood," Condi shares. "But I thought of the Civil Rights Movement as part of a struggle to give all Americans the opportunity to pursue whatever interests them most, where they can best use their talents. Because I viewed the struggle of black America as meaning the right of each of us to do what we are best equipped to do, it did not seem to me to be a disjunction for me to follow my own particular course. Rather the reverse—I was exercising a fundamental right of Americans."[2]

Raised in the War Zone

On December 1, 1955, Condoleezza was barely one year old. Approximately a hundred miles south of her home, in Montgomery, Alabama, an African-American seamstress and secretary of the National Association for the Advancement of Colored People (NAACP) was advocating for the rights of blacks to be treated equally. Although Condi would never meet the then twenty-one-year-old Rosa Parks, the seamstress's stand against racism would help pave the way for the toddler in the years to come.

Parks said that her rebellion was spurred by the fact that she was tired—tired of alleged inferiority, tired of segregation, and tired of prejudice. Her simple act of defiance and her refusal to obey bus driver James Blake's demand that she give up her seat to a white passenger led to her arrest and her trial for an act of civil disobedience and would fuel a locomotive of action that would move the Civil Rights Movement into high speed.

While white supremacists called for Rosa Parks to be punished to the full extent of the law, her act of disobedience against segregation triggered a 381-day bus boycott and the most successful mass movement against racial segregation in history, launching the victorious civil rights ministry and career of Martin Luther King, Jr., as the face and leader of the Civil Rights Movement. While King had accepted the pastorate of the Dexter Avenue Baptist Church in Montgomery, Alabama the same year, he was already a strong worker for civil rights for members of his race. By this time he was a member of the executive committee of the NAACP, the leading organization of its kind in the nation. During the days of the boycott, King was arrested, his home was bombed, and he was subjected to personal abuse. Regardless of the assaults against him, King stood strong in his faith and in his vision to retain equal rights.

Racial tensions were triggered by the boycott and brought with it immeasurable amounts of verbal and violent physical assaults against the black race. Burning crosses, bombs, assaults, murders, and house burnings permeated Birmingham. In response, blacks held marches, sit-ins, and protests, many of which were televised and were viewed by Condoleezza with her parents. While her father would not participate in the blatant obstinacy and defiance against racism, he did take his daughter to watch some of the protests.

When Condi asked her parents and other family members about prejudice, she got the same answer every time. "It's not your problem," they'd say. "Don't worry about it." On the other side of the coin, however, they also told her that she had to be "twice as good" as whites to be on the same playing field. Her father counseled her that the way out of racism was to "fight with your mind," something his father had taught him years earlier.

Condi was further told that whites who hate blacks would always try to keep the black race within the confines of a negative stereotype but that she didn't have to submit to them. "Though Birmingham had its limits," Condi remembers, "my parents told me that Birmingham's limits were not mine."[1]

To help Condi overcome racism, develop her dreams, and see no limit on attaining them, her parents surrounded her with adults who rose above prejudice and were successful in various fields. Lori White, a friend of Condi, says the two of them talk often about those days in her life.

"Both of her parents raised her with a strong understanding of what it meant to be an African-American in this country, but also telling her that other people's view of the limitations of what an African-American might be able to achieve should not stop her from having the widest and highest dreams possible. They both wanted her to make sure that she was proud of her African-American heritage, without allowing that pride to elevate her above others. She was encouraged to not allow others, particularly Southerners at that time who believed there were things African-Americans couldn't do or shouldn't aspire to do, to stop her, for example, from attending particular schools or from shopping at particular kinds of places. So her parents made sure that she had ever-present African-American role models who allowed her to understand what she could aspire to be."

White goes on, "For example, typically you have bifurcation between the middle class and affluent African-Americans and those who are much less affluent. So if I'm a poor African-American person growing up in today's society, a black doctor does not live in my community, and so I do not have that role model present to me, but that was something that Condi was able to experience growing up in Birmingham."

Condi says, "I do not believe [race] has limited who I am or what I can become. And that's because I had parents who, while telling me what it meant to be African-American and exposing me to that, also allowed me to develop as an individual to be who I wanted to be."[2]

Condi's parents also encouraged and pushed their daughter to be good at everything she did and exposed her to and enrolled her in all the activities and classes to which white children on the other side of town had access.

"My parents were very strategic," Condi says in relation to discrimination. "I was going to be so prepared, and I was going to do all of these things that were revered in white society so well, that I would be armored somehow from racism. I would be able to confront white society on its own terms."[3]

No matter what her parents did, however, they couldn't completely shield Condi from the prejudice that she'd see on the news as she watched beating after beating of blacks by police who were paid in part by the tax dollars of blacks to protect them. And although her parents and others in her inner circle of family and friends were extraordinary role models who encouraged her to be all she could be, others expected little or nothing from her.

"I grew up in Birmingham, Alabama, a place that was once described, with no exaggeration, as the most thoroughly segregated city in the country. I know what it means to hold dreams and aspirations when half your neighbors think of you as incapable of, or uninterested in, anything higher."[4]

Condi did excel at everything she put her mind to. Thus she remembers her childhood with great fondness despite the hatred that drenched the city like a torrid rain during the late fifties and sixties.

"It's almost like quoting from Dickens," she says about the trying years of the civil rights era and her extraordinary childhood with parents who were so loving and supportive. "'It was the best of times, it was the worst of times.' The worst of it was the feeling of almost civil war. It was frightening for children my age."[5]

It was a terrifying time for all blacks. Entire families were killed by bombs placed by the Ku Klux Klan, and every attempt to stand for their rights was met with opposition. Instead of protecting them, the law advocated against them. It didn't matter what the Constitution said—it was ignored by elected individuals paid to make sure it was upheld. Whites even went so far as to say that some blacks preferred to be inferior because they hadn't resisted segregation for hundreds of years. Condi disagrees. "Given a choice between tyranny and freedom, people will choose freedom. People want the best for their children and they want their creativity and their hard work to be rewarded. People want the freedom to speak their minds, to choose those who will lead them and the right to embrace their faith."[6]

Birmingham continued to be a vortex of prejudice, infested with the Ku Klux Klan and permeated by what is not so fondly referred to as the Jim Crow era, a movement that spread hatred for blacks as if it were a highly contagious disease incapable of being contained, let alone stopped. Named after a popular nineteenth-century minstrel song, the Jim Crow era stereotyped African-Americans as useless and ignorant. Thus *Jim Crow* came to exemplify a system of government-sanctioned racial oppression and segregation in the United States. Furthermore, the phrase *Jim Crow* became a racial slur for all who had dark or colored skin and was part of an extended vocabulary used by prejudiced whites, including various slang words and racial slurs with which we are all, sadly, too familiar.

The Jim Crow laws originated from the Black Codes that were enforced in America from 1865 to 1866. The laws sprouted up in the late nineteenth century after Reconstruction and lasted until well into the 1960s, when Condi was in her pre-teens.

The Jim Crow era was a time of great tribulation for everyone involved. For the black victims it included extensive violence, discrimination, poverty, and for many death. For black sympathizers who were set to challenge what had become standard mistreatment of blacks, it was a time of great opposition and resistance.

Prejudiced whites kept the hatred spinning out of control with racial slurs, unprovoked beatings, continual uprisings, and unwarranted deaths. By the time Condoleezza was one year old, nearly five thousand blacks had reportedly been lynched nationwide since the early 1800s, many in the Jones Valley, which today includes the city of Birmingham.[7]

To add fuel to the fire, the U.S. Supreme Court rulings favored the Jim Crow segregation laws, not only *allowing* the separation of whites from blacks but *encouraging* it. The goal of the Ku Klux Klan—to dispose of the entire black race—was supported by the governing leaders of America even though the Constitution blatantly contradicted their stance.

Despite the hatred that infected their surroundings, John Rice adamantly read and quoted the Bible to Condoleezza. He reassured her that her identity was not defined by white men in white robes who told America that blacks were worthless, disposable, and a danger and hindrance to society. Instead, he told her, she was fearfully and wonderfully made in the image of God, she was his child, and her value was immeasurable. He also affirmed to her that God's plan was not the same as man's and that God had purposely created her the way she was—color and all.

Condi loved it when her father would share stories from the Bible, specifically in relation to the Israelites, whom God had delivered from slavery under the leadership of Moses and Joshua. She knew some of the stories of her great-grandparents who had endured beatings and oppression far beyond what Birmingham was experiencing, and she inherited their passion for democracy at all costs. Deliverance from slavery was a promise God had made and kept to her forefathers, but still one that remained unfulfilled in many ways. It was a promise her grandparents and great-grandparents had invested faith in, but a vow they would not see come into complete fruition in their lifetime. Still, they knew they were fighting for the generations to follow, and Condi would be a recipient of their perseverance, patience, and prayers.

Faith in God had been the cornerstone of the black culture for hundreds of years and was the predominant root of Condoleezza's family. The church was not only a place of worship but was also a social, economic, political, and educational outlet. The church *was* their family and served as a shelter in the midst of the most brutal racial assaults. For young boys and girls like Condi, it became the place outside of home where they gained reassurance of their identity, hope, and worth.

During both the oppression of slavery and the segregation of America, church buildings were often used secondarily as schools to educate black children because legislated racism and hatred in America drastically affected and often prevented blacks from attending schools that were readily accessible to white America, especially for extended education.

In the rare cases when African-Americans were granted admission into a college, they were often ostracized by the faculty and other students. Some blacks backed down and succumbed to the racism, accepting what they believed was their fate; but many blacks kicked against the goads of prejudice and fought harder for equal rights. Condi's relatives were fighters. But white America still sat on the throne of injustice, demanding segregation and supremacy. Four years before Condi's birth an African-American man was denied admission to the state-supported University of Texas Law School solely because he was black.[8] During that same year an African-American citizen of Oklahoma, possessing a Master's degree, was admitted to the Graduate School of the state-supported University of Oklahoma as a candidate for a doctorate in education but was required to sit in a segregated row in class and at a special table in the library and cafeteria.[9]

Slowly but surely black Americans sought legal counsel and began to challenge the blatant contradiction between the Constitution and the legislated racism that disregarded and overruled the founding documents.

Landmark changes began to occur that liberated the African-American community and infuriated racists as they began to lose power and control over the demoralizing laws separating blacks from whites. Realizing they didn't have a leg to stand on within the court system, these prejudiced men began to beef up their resistance outside the law. In collaboration with other race-hating assemblies like the Ku Klux Klan, they continued to search for opportunities to restrict, dehumanize, intimidate, and kill blacks through scare tactics and unwarranted beatings and murders. It was life-threatening for black Americans to be alone on the streets even during the day, and many traveled in pairs or groups to maintain their safety. When night fell, many would not leave their homes for fear of being kidnapped, beaten, or killed.

In the summer of 1955, fourteen-year-old Emmett Louis "Bobo" Till was sent to stay with his great-uncle, Moses Wright, who lived in Money, Mississippi. A few days after he arrived, he joined other teenagers as they went to Bryant's Grocery and Meat Market to get some candy. While in the store, Till allegedly whistled at or openly flirted with Carolyn Bryant. When her husband, twenty-four-year-old Roy Bryant, got word of the incident several days later upon his return from an out-of-town trip, he was livid and decided that he and his half-brother, J.W. Milam, thirty-six, would meet around 2:00 A.M. on the following Sunday, August 28, to "teach the boy a lesson."

Bryant and Milam kidnapped Till from his uncle's house and drove him to a weathered plantation shed in a neighboring county, where they brutally beat him until he was unrecognizable, cut off an ear, gouged out an eye, then shot him with a .45 caliber pistol before tying a seventy-five-pound cotton gin fan around his neck with barbed wire. Afterward he was dropped into the Tallahatchie River near another small town.

The brothers were arrested the following day after staying with relatives just miles away from where the murder took place and were indicted on September 6. They were later acquitted by an all-white jury. They later confessed and boasted about committing the murder in a *Look* magazine interview, for a modest sum of money.

In 1957 Martin Luther King, Jr., along with Charles K. Steele and Fred L. Shuttlesworth, established the Southern Christian Leadership Conference (SCLC), of which King was made the first president. The organization was formed to provide new leadership for the now rapidly growing Civil Rights Movement. King built the organization on the principles and ethics of Christianity, but its operational techniques came from Mahatma Gandhi, the political and spiritual leader of India and the Indian Independence Movement. Considered the "father" of India, Gandhi pioneered resistance through mass civil disobedience strongly founded upon nonviolence at all costs.

King adopted Gandhi's nonviolent practice. After his house had been bombed and he had been attacked and sent to jail, friends and family greeted him at his house armed with guns and clubs, but he told them to return home with their weapons, saying that the Civil Rights Movement would be fought with the love of God, not with weapons of the world—namely, retribution and hate.

Based in Atlanta, the all-black organization's main objective was to coordinate and assist local agencies working for the full equality of African-Americans. The new organization was committed to using nonviolence in the struggle for civil rights, and SCLC adopted the motto "Not one hair of one head of one person should be harmed," a slogan they derived from the Bible (Luke 21:18).

In contrast to that motto against nonviolence, a white mob beat Shuttlesworth with whips, baseball bats, and chains during an attempt to enroll his daughters Pat and Ricky in an all-white public school. Ironically, the day of Shuttlesworth's beating (September 9, 1957) was the day President Eisenhower signed the 1957 Civil Rights Act.

Although Birmingham raged out of control with racism and demonstrations against black Americans during Condi's formative years, her parents lived on the quiet side of the Civil Rights Movement. Despite John's continual interaction and friendships with major civil rights leaders such as Fred Shuttlesworth (an activist who led the fight against racism and established the Alabama Christian Movement for Human Rights) and Dr. Ralph David Abernathy (a partner of Martin Luther King and second-in-charge during King's participation in the Southern Christian Leadership Conference), he was not an active protestor—he did not participate in marches and demonstrations as did his friends. Instead he chose to fight prejudice by empowering and mentoring young African-Americans through one-on-one mentoring and relationships—and Condi was his primary protégé.

Because of his deep convictions of faith and the depth of their father-daughter bond, Condi never remembers feeling scared within the walls of her own home. Instead she felt safe and protected by her father. Her parents talked openly and honestly with her about life and the best way to combat its difficulties and specifically racism—through faith and education.

In 1957, in conjunction with pastoring Westminster Presbyterian Church, John also became a counselor for the Alabama State Employment Service and a guidance counselor for the Birmingham Public School. In both roles he provided guidance, mentoring, and instruction.

Meanwhile, in Little Rock, Arkansas nine black students were blocked from entering all-white Central High School on the orders of the Governor, Orval Faubus. The uproar caused President Eisenhower to send federal troops and the National Guard to Arkansas to intervene on behalf of the students, who become known as the Little Rock Nine. Integration continued to be a violent transition for many blacks.

As an only child Condi matured quickly. And since both her parents were educators, the priority in their home was learning above all else. Angelena personally took time after teaching school all day to teach Condi to read and write.

While her parents were at work during the day, Condi stayed with her Grandma Ray, watching her teach person after person how to play the piano. It stirred something in the three-year-old—a desire to learn to play herself. She says she'd go to her grandmother's piano and bang on the keys, trying to emulate what she saw her grandmother teaching other kids.

Her grandmother approached Angelena, telling her that she thought they needed to teach Condi how to play the piano. Angelena thought she was too young. Not too long after that, Condi boldly asked her parents for her own piano. They told her that if she learned to play, they'd get her one. The next time she was at her grandmother's, she asked her to teach her to play the piano, and her grandmother agreed. That day Grandma Ray spent eight hours teaching Condi to play the song "What a Friend We Have in Jesus."

"My grandmother taught me that song because she and my grandfather were people of faith and, like my parents, wanted me to have a firm foundation in Christ. That night, after I spent eight hours learning the song, I played it for my parents."[10]

As she played for them, John and Angelena knew what they had to do. They immediately borrowed the money, and the following weekend they went out and rented a piano for the young protégé to learn on. Ironically, the second song Condi learned was the hymn "Amazing Grace," written by John Newton, a commander of an English slave ship. Newton experienced what he later described as a "great deliverance" during a severe storm during a trip home from the coast of Sierra Leone, Africa. He gave his life to Jesus, stepped down from his role as captain of the ship, and worked as a tide surveyor while he studied for the ministry. He spent the remainder of his forty-three years of life preaching the gospel of Jesus Christ. At eighty-two Newton said, "My memory is nearly gone, but I remember two things, that I am a great sinner, and that Christ is a great Saviour."[11]

Immediately Condi began taking lessons from both her grandmother and her mother (both played for various church choirs). She sat on a stack of hymnals until she was big enough to reach the keys, and she could read music fluently before her feet could touch the pedals and before she could read books. Annye Marie Downing remembers those days clearly: "Condi would accompany her mother on the piano for the Chancel Choir at our church, and that child could play. It was amazing how fast she learned. Everyone was impressed."

Condi seemed to be a prodigy in just about every area from the beginning. She whizzed through kindergarten with no problems when she was barely four. When Angelena enrolled Condi in first grade, two months shy of being five, the principal of the school refused to allow her to attend, saying she wasn't old enough.

Determined to allow her daughter to learn at her own pace and not as dictated by school guidelines, Angelena took a year off from work and homeschooled Condoleezza. As a result, Condi was able to skip first grade, and when she did enroll in school she went directly into second grade. Angelena had accomplished her desired goal—she just had to take a different route to get there.

Angelena knew when Condi was very young that she was gifted intellectually. To support her belief and to see exactly where her daughter was in comparison to other children, she took her daughter to the Southern University in Baton Rouge, Louisiana for psychological testing. Condi was found to be a genius with an extraordinarily high IQ. Both parents knew they needed to build on the intellect that God had graciously given to their daughter.

Angelena joined a book club and began to feed Condi's mind with various topics. Recreational reading was not the goal but rather assigned reading that further matured the child. She found out through supplying these books that Condi loved to read about history, especially World War II and biblical history. So she'd specifically try to find books for her daughter on her apparent two loves. As a result of all her reading, Condi had a lot of questions.

"Part of the foundation of my upbringing was a mutual respect between my parents and me, evident in the freedom to ask and engage in questions all the time. Since my father was a Presbyterian minister and my mother a woman of faith, questions always came up centered around the Bible, specifically, historical Jesus. So I grew up asking questions and getting sound answers."[12]

John too encouraged Condi to read. He bought her comic books that were historical to help feed the fire that burned inside the youngster. Condi says her favorite book as a child was an introduction to great composers, full of biographical information on extraordinary composers of the past. John also encouraged Condi to find a sport to participate and excel in. Thus she began taking ice skating lessons.

After she began school in the public system Condi also fell in love with chemistry and science. She was stimulated by the intricacy and depth of the subjects. Although she got straight A's in school, she says that math was her worst subject. Having difficulty in school wasn't a serious issue for Condi, but it was for other kids in her community. So along with other parents and teachers John and Angelena went out of their way to help their child and others succeed. John orchestrated several teachers to come to his church on Tuesday and Thursday nights and on Saturdays during the day to tutor struggling students, so no child would be left behind in the school system and so every black child would be educated.

"It was in the very air we breathed that education was the way out," says Condi. "The teachers were so dedicated. They lived and worked with the dream that the future was with the children. They worked Saturdays, they took kids to concerts at their own expense, they made the best of the substandard facilities they were allotted. Both my parents were teachers in the public school, so I had the extra advantage of also being taught at home."[13]

"The bonding together of the black community was inspiring," she also says. "We all helped each other. Class differences in the black community had no meaning. We were bonded together. The dedication of the teachers in the black schools was awe-inspiring. They worked so hard to give the kids the very best they could manage, in spite of the wretched facilities we had. In my science class, with 18 students, there were three battered microscopes, but the teachers made the difference."[14]

Black teachers *were* extraordinary in the forties throughout the sixties, dealing with unjust treatment continually. They were expected to teach more students for about 60 percent of the salary of white teachers. In 1944 there were 42.8 black students versus 24.3 white students per teacher. Even after a 1947 lawsuit equalizing salaries, black teachers continued to pay for their own classroom materials while white teachers received extra funds from the school board. In the 1950s the average class size was forty-eight black students compared to thirty-five in white schools. That same year

Alabama spent $120 on each white child, but only $60 per black pupil.[15]

The extra effort that teachers and the church provided for black kids gave many of them motivation and the feeling that they must succeed—after all, everybody in their community was counting on it and investing in it.

"The entire black community was determined on one thing," said Rice. "It was that as America emerged from the old ways of intolerance and prejudice, the children would be ready to take their rightful place in American society. Among all my friends, the kids I grew up with, there was, for example, no doubt in our minds that we would grow up and go to colleges—integrated colleges—just like other Americans."[16]

"Even under segregation there was a strength of community and a strength of spirit," Condi says. "Life was very pleasant for children coming from my background, but there was always tension between what was possible in Birmingham and what you felt should be possible in America. . . .

"We were raised with an expectation that when access to the privileges only white people then enjoyed was available, we were going to be prepared to take advantage of it. The will to succeed in America was absolutely critical, and you owed it to your community to succeed. We were all reared with a strong sense of responsibility to the community and to those who didn't make it out. We can't squander opportunities. If I fail, I don't just fail for me. I fail and disappoint all the people who made it possible for me to do what I'm doing—and all the people who are looking up to me to watch how well I'm doing it."[17]

The Rices continued to stimulate diversity in Condi's mind as she grew and willingly drove her to her dance classes, language lessons, and various sports activities including tennis and ice-skating—all of which she excelled in.

Condoleezza's astonishing developmental abilities surprised everyone *but* her parents. From birth, both parents knew their daughter was special, unique, and irreplaceable, regularly telling others and Condi that she didn't belong to them but to God, and that it was God working through her that enabled her to accomplish so much in such a short amount of time. To them, their daughter's success at virtually everything she did was a confirmation of what they believed God had told them and what they had invested in from the beginning.

Condi was thrown into the performing arts arena at an early age. She began doing piano recitals and performances in public for the first time when she was four at a tea for new teachers in the Birmingham public school system. It went so well that Condi was asked time and time again to perform at various functions throughout town. In addition to the piano, she learned to play the flute and violin.

The child fell in love with classical music and aspired to be a classical pianist from as early as she remembers, studying Bach and Mozart religiously. When Condi was five years of age, her mother gave her a recording of the four-act opera *Aida* by Giuseppe Verdi, with the Italian libretto by Antonio Ghislanzoni. The opera was rich in heritage and meaning for the young prodigy. Verdi's opus was originally written by French Egyptologist Auguste Mariette and had first been performed at the Khedivial Opera House in Cairo on Christmas Eve 1871. The opera was met with great acclaim when it opened and continues to this day to be a staple of the standard operatic repertoire. For Condi, it successfully stimulated her desire to pursue a career in the performing arts, something she'd hold onto tightly for many years to come.

THE ADOLESCENT YEARS

*S*undays in Condi's family meant church. As a matter of fact, the church was the center of their lives, not only because John was a pastor, but because the church played a crucial role in the life of the black community as a whole. In black churches people were encouraged to persevere through hardships in life because they would be rewarded in the next one. But religious institutions were also the center of the community's social, civic, and even economic development. Black pastors were recognized spokespersons for the community, and church organizations such as credit unions and mutual aid societies were the backbone of black civic and humanitarian services. Fellowship with other black Americans of faith in the environment of the church also provided for many of their other needs—socially, educationally, and otherwise. Historically, children of that era were often raised with the mentality that this was a community effort, and everyone involved in the child's life was responsible to impart wisdom and counsel to him or her. As a result, Condi had many positive spiritual influences in her childhood.

Condi's earliest memories are of Sunday school, interacting with other kids and learning Bible stories through dance and song. Her religious beliefs, like those of her parents and those in many other faith-based denominations, held that God is the supreme authority throughout the universe, that his purpose for them is seen in the Bible—particularly what is revealed in the New Testament through the life of Jesus Christ—and that salvation is God's generous gift to all sinners and not the result of one's own accomplishments.

As a result of their own convictions in faith, Condi's parents taught her to trust and believe in God, a belief she says she's never questioned or doubted once since. Additionally they taught her early in life that she could depend on the Lord to guide and lead her. This was especially helpful during the difficult times in life yet to come. So at a very young age Condi knew without question that she was never alone and could always rely on her faith to get her through any difficult moment. Even though the external world around her was in chaos, she knew she could have internal peace from trusting in Jesus.

To Condi, her father was her ultimate hero, and she credits him for her spiritual development at such a young age. "My father was an enormous influence in my spiritual life. He was a theologian, a doctor of divinity. He was someone who let you argue about things. He didn't say, 'Just accept it.' And when I had questions, which we all do, he encouraged that.

"I [liked] that because my father didn't brush aside my questions about faith. He allowed me as someone who lives in my mind to also live in my faith."[1]

John Rice was known to be a man of prayer. Those who remember him best say that he would not leave his home to run errands without praying first. He prayed by himself, with his wife, and with his daughter every chance he got. He prayed for and with those he mentored, his students, and those he counseled at the school. He ultimately invested in four things: God, his family, education, and liberation for blacks—in that order.

Just as her father was influential in her spiritual life, her mother taught her how to be a lady and gave her daughter a sense of class and style. Angelena was always dressed from the nicest stores in Birmingham (predominantly frequented by whites), and she always dressed Condoleezza impeccably. Angelena was known to take her daughter to the finest and most exclusive children's stores in Birmingham and willingly paid the exorbitant prices to dress herself and her daughter in the same clothes to which whites had access. Ignoring the glares and stares, Angelena acted like they belonged there just as much as they did.

Ironically, the Rices were considered upper-class in the black echelons of society—not because of money but because of education. And although money was not in abundance, a humble pride was. Angelena always wore the finest clothes, tailored and pressed perfectly, and also dressed Condi in the finest they could afford.

Both John and Angelena taught Condi to "confront white society on its own terms," and while that statement encompassed education, it also included appearance.

Condi has told the story on numerous occasions about the time her mother took her to a store where the saleslady insisted that Condi try on her clothes in a storage room rather than in the whites-only dressing room. Angelena told the salesperson that under no terms would her daughter try on her clothes in the storage room; otherwise she would take her daughter and the saleswoman's commission elsewhere. The saleswoman gave in to Angelena's confrontation, but not without fear of being caught and fired.

In another story Condi often shares regarding her mother's confrontation with racism, they were in a fine dress store that sold hats. When Condi touched one, the saleslady scolded her. In her daughter's defense, Angelena encouraged Condi to touch every hat in the store—and she happily obeyed.

Angelena's stance against racism left an imprint on the young girl's heart. Angelena wasn't afraid to stand up for herself or her daughter, and her example fortified the esteem of Condi so that she too would have the strength to stand on her own someday.

From early on in Condi's life, she and her parents were close. Multiple people who have known them Condi's entire life say that the Rices were a unique threesome and had a bond that no one could penetrate. Condi agrees. "My parents and I were always close. I was their only child and their constant companion, a role they took seriously. They invested time, faith, knowledge, love, and passion into my life."[2]

Despite the fact that seldom a day went by during Condi's formative years when blacks weren't haunted by rebel yells in the daylight hours, terrorized by night riders and burning crosses, and accused of burning their own homes, Condi says her childhood was good. "Despite my fond memories of Birmingham as a place where I was, as a child, secure, I also remember a place called 'Bombingham'—where I witnessed the denial of democracy in America for so many years. It was, after all, the city of Bull Connor and the Ku Klux Klan."[3] Bombs were going off regularly. Between 1940 and 1960 nearly fifty unresolved, racially directed bombings occurred in Birmingham.[4] As a result of these demonstrations of hate, Condi's father and other black men from the neighborhood formed a brigade at the entrance to their cul-de-sac and with guns loaded prepared to protect their families at all costs. Alma Powell, wife of former Chairman of the Joint Chiefs of Staff and U.S. Secretary of State Colin Powell, recalls her father doing this as well in Birmingham. Because of her father's need to protect his family, Condi openly shares her view on the Second Amendment—the right to bear arms.

Still, civil rights fighters knew that the real battle wasn't at the end of the street where they each had their homes but in the courts where there were conflicting laws. One law gave liberty; the other refused it. These seemingly contradictory laws fought relentlessly against each other through the conflicting races—for some blacks the penalty for protesting segregation was often violent assault and at times death. For Condi's father's friend, Fred Shuttlesworth, life and death hung in the balance on a day-to-day basis.

Shuttlesworth was a good friend of John Rice. They talked often about the race wars at hand and how they could combat them individually and as a group. At the ripe age of twenty-three

Shuttlesworth had his first pastorate, but he quickly realized that his calling from God was not to preach but to lead by example against the sin of prejudice. As a result of fulfilling that calling, he was arrested over thirty-five times and was instrumental throughout the Civil Rights Movement for filing or defending over forty lawsuits for the cause. In the midst of his fight he established the Alabama Christian Movement for Human Rights (ACMHR) in May 1956. White supremacists hated Shuttlesworth and attempted to take his life on several occasions. In one attempt the Ku Klux Klan blew up his home with sixteen sticks of dynamite.

"When I heard the thunderous explosion, I knew exactly what it was: a bomb with my name on it," remembers Shuttlesworth. "It was Christmas night of 1956, and I was the pastor of the Bethel Baptist Church in Birmingham, Alabama. The local black citizens had endured so much of the Ku Klux Klan's dynamite that our city was known as 'Bombingham.' But this was my first (though not my last) bomb. It had gone off right next to the bed I was lying in. The wall behind my head shattered, and the ceiling caved in around me. For some reason, a happy, peaceful feeling came over me. The 27th Psalm kept running through my head: 'The Lord is my light and my salvation; whom shall I fear?'

"My house, which adjoined the church, was nearly demolished, but I walked out of the wreckage without a hair on my head disturbed. My wife and children were also unmarked. . . . I feel that I must take the opportunity here to stress what is often lost in the retelling of the civil rights struggle. And that is the faith and determination of ordinary folks caught up in a national moral crisis. During the Birmingham campaign, thousands of people, old and young, attended the mass meetings that were held in local black churches virtually every night for five weeks. We prayed, we collected money, we teased the white policemen who had been sent there to spy on us. As the preachers got warmed up, the spiritual energy got hotter and hotter. Both the source and the reflection of our soaring strength and unity was our music. The songs—'I'm on

My Way to Freedom Land,' 'Oh, Freedom Over Me,' 'Ain't Gonna Let Nobody Turn Me Around'—bound us into a whole that allowed us to accomplish feats we never would have been able to pull off as individuals and turned us into agents of what Dr. King liked to call 'soul force.' . . . The civil rights revolution was a battle, yes, but it was also a profound spiritual transformation, not only of a people but of a nation."[5]

Currently in his mid-eighties, Shuttlesworth remembers the days of the Civil Rights Movement as if they had just happened and can tell story after story of the assaults on his life. Shuttlesworth boldly states that he endured the verbal and physical abuse from whites because of his religious convictions and because he was called by God through the Holy Spirit to advocate for liberation. In doing so, he endured ruthless beatings with whips and chains, bombings on his home, and relentless attacks on his family. Firefighters used a powerful stream of water from a hose to pin him against the wall of the 16th Street Baptist Church, after which he was hospitalized.

Shuttlesworth compares his suffering with that of the apostle Paul. "Abuse was my calling," he said. "The Apostle Paul suffered knowing it was for a higher purpose, and so did I. God knew what He was doing, so I followed His lead."

John Rice and Fred Shuttlesworth had a lot in common, specifically in the area of education. Like Condi's father, Shuttlesworth had climbed the ladder of higher education and was a graduate from Selma University and Alabama State College. He also felt strongly about mentorship—John's expertise and forte. He knew that youth were the future, and whatever strides and accomplishments he made, the baton would need to be handed to a younger generation. So Shuttlesworth took it upon himself to mentor John, knowing that he mentored youth effectively. He felt that if he could impact John, he could impact the world through America's youth. Shuttlesworth's and John's soapbox was the solidity found in the gospel of Jesus Christ revealed in the Bible, upon which the Constitution of the United States was built. Thus Shuttlesworth and

John felt they were only fulfilling the promise that God had given our forefathers long ago. Condi agrees with this logic.

"Throughout the South, when I was growing up," Condi says, "the organized cruelty of segregation was embodied in custom, encompassed in law, and enforced through brutality. Nevertheless, our Founding Fathers had dug the well of democracy deep in America. They believed that no act of God or fact of nature condemned one man to be the instrument of another. Our Founders knew that human beings are imperfect, so they enshrined certain natural rights in our democratic institutions. The only problem, of course, was that when the Founding Fathers said, 'We the people,' they didn't mean me.

"Nonetheless, the ideal of justice at the heart of this regime was the mirror that black Americans held in the face of their oppressors. This reflected a stark choice for our entire country: Either the principles of our nation's Creed were true for everyone—or they were true for no one. If these truths were indeed self-evident—if all men really were created equal—then it was America that had to change, not America's democratic ideals."[6]

While many whites separated themselves from blacks because they thought themselves to be superior, many in the African-American community purposely avoided whites to avoid confrontation and racism. As a result many black children of that era grew up without even seeing a white person until they were adults. Condi remembers the first time she ever saw a white man. She was about four years old and was placed on the lap of a white Santa during Christmastime. In the picture taken then, she's looking up at the red and white dressed figure as if there is something remotely wrong with him and the situation in which she found herself.

"I [was] looking at Santa Claus with extraordinary suspicion," she says. "And I told my father that's probably because he was the first white person I had ever seen. You went through your entire day, your entire life, and never came into contact with anyone of another race."[7]

In 1960, to bring in the New Year, fifteen hundred people gathered at 16th Street Baptist Church to celebrate an Emancipation Day Program, which celebrated President Abraham Lincoln's Emancipation Proclamation freeing slaves. In the months that followed, sit-ins by black college students at local white lunch counters were frequent despite verbal and physical abuse and arrests. In a four-month period of time, more than fifty thousand black students and white sympathizers held sit-ins in seventy-eight cities.[8] As a result, riots and violence broke out on every building block that blacks tried to cement in a foundation of liberation.

In the 1960 presidential election campaign, John F. Kennedy argued for a new Civil Rights Act to help minorities get equal rights. After the successful election, it was discovered that over 70 percent of the African-American vote went to Kennedy, but he failed to keep his campaign promise. This outraged blacks who had voted for him based on his vow to help them. They knew they needed partners in the government to help remove unjust obstacles that were hindering the process. Although President Kennedy didn't follow through promptly as he promised, judges, lawmakers, and bureaucrats, realizing that the blacks were not going to back down, began to step up to the plate and do their part.

"They set new judicial precedents and passed new legislation and enforced our just demands, even at the point of a bayonet in places like Little Rock and Ole Miss, [and] along the bus routes of the Deep South," Condi remembers. "But make no mistake: Citizenship was not a gift that was given to black Americans. It was a right that was won through the courage and sacrifice of many impatient patriots, weary of hypocrisy, whose demand was 'freedom now.'"[9]

Four of those impatient patriots were black students from a local college who on February 1 began a sit-in at a segregated Woolworth's lunch counter. The students were refused service but were allowed to stay at the counter. The sit-in triggered many similar events throughout the South. As Condi learned about the sit-ins, her father told her that although she couldn't have a hamburger at Woolworth's, she was smarter than all the people who were stopping her from doing so, and she could be anything she wanted—including President of the United States.

THE NORMAL AMERICAN FAMILY

Like many American families, when school was out over the summer, the Rices would go on vacation together. John, Angelena, and Condi loved to drive their car out of state, and John was known to do whatever he could to meet the needs of his two favorite girls. During one summer trip it was so hot for the girls that he pulled over and had a mechanic install air-conditioning so they would be more comfortable on their journey. This was at a time when few cars had air-conditioning, let alone those owned by black families.

Condi remembers her vacations as times of education as they often visited college campuses. On one such trip, John attended a summer program at Columbia University, and he and Angelena were able to take Condi to Coney Island. Ironically, blacks were not welcome at Birmingham's amusement park except on one day out of the season. So the Rices took advantage of opportunities as they traveled.

There wasn't a hotel between Birmingham and Washington that allowed blacks to stay overnight. So when they headed east, the twelve-hour ride was often a long, drawn-out one for the family. During these trips John and Angelena put their daughter in charge of the distribution of the meals they would pick up on the go. Condi took the role seriously and would have her parents "order" their food from her and the "store" she imagined she ran from the backseat. There was only one rule that Condi implemented in running her store—no one could eat when she was sleeping. The store was closed for business during that time.

Several times the Rices' vacation was spent in Denver, Colorado, where her parents would attend various educational programs and tour the campus of the University of Denver. Condi would often spend her days taking ice-skating lessons or practicing. She was fond of Denver because it had indoor skating year-round.

Back on the home front in Birmingham, Condi had been taking piano lessons for two years with her rented piano and was so good that she was accompanying her mother to the organ bench during worship services at church almost every Sunday.

Unlike many adolescents, Condi was always well-mannered and well-behaved. She was taught to sit quietly and respect her elders, even when other children were unruly—she was taught to be the example. Thus she would often sit quietly in a room of misbehaving children and repeatedly ask politely for her work. She has been frequently described by her family and their friends as "an adult in a child's body."

Condi's many uncles and aunts were active in her life and were supportive of her, encouraging her and investing time to help her in her varying interests. One family member she was especially close to was her Uncle Alto. Alto was Angelena's youngest brother and was a good-looking man. His continual doting and favor on the young Condoleezza created a girlish crush on him. Lori White, a friend and prior colleague of Condi, laughs as she relays the story.

"Condi had a huge crush on her uncle when she was a little girl. And when Connie (his future wife) appeared in the picture, Condi was really jealous. And she said when [her] Uncle Alto would come calling, she would sit between Connie and [her] Uncle Alto! When they were getting married and Connie was preparing her trousseau, she bought a nightgown for Condi. Once she did that, Condi was like, 'Now she incurred my favor by buying that for me—so now she was okay by me!'"

Condi's jealousy was calmed with a gift from her future aunt—a woman who, no doubt, knew the girl well and the best way to smolder a potential fire.

In the meantime, the battle against segregation continued to get more heated. John's friend and mentor Fred Shuttlesworth became a civil rights figure that Birmingham blacks could rely on and look up to, someone in their own neck of the woods. In 1961 Shuttlesworth helped the Congress on Racial Equality (CORE) organize its Freedom Rides and led mass demonstrations against segregation in Birmingham. Bull Connor's wrath struck back full-force, which resulted in Shuttlesworth's being hospitalized on various occasions.

Ironically, at around the same time President John F. Kennedy established the Peace Corps, an independent but Congress-supported federal agency designed to promote mutual understanding and peace between Americans and the outside world—all while America was in chaos within.

Condi was eight years old when she began to really see American racism for what it was—two different societies trying to function within the walls of one nation. During that time the civil rights activists and teachers began encouraging school-age children to march in the demonstrations. When the kids did so, at Bull Connor's request they were fire-hosed and chased by vicious Birmingham Police Department dogs. Emergency rooms looked like a war zone because of the many casualties, and no one in the government who could do something about it seemed to care. The media outlets, predominantly owned and run by whites, made no attempt to intervene but were more than willing to film what was going on for the world to see.

Condi's father agreed with the *goals* of the Civil Rights Movement but not the *means*. He could not conceive how anyone would put his or her child at risk—even for equal rights. He encouraged schoolchildren who were being encouraged to become advocates in the civil rights fight not to get involved in the demonstrations, though he did take Condi downtown to watch them. Condi sat high above the ground on her father's broad shoulders as he walked up and down the fairgrounds where many of the young adults who had been attending his church and Youth Night had been confined after being arrested for demonstrating. He made sure they were not harmed and had their needs met.

On May 4, 1961 CORE began sending student volunteers on bus trips to test the newly implemented laws prohibiting segregation in interstate travel facilities. One of the first two groups of Freedom Riders traveled from Washington, D.C. to New Orleans in an attempt to confront the system's own contradictions. A little over two weeks into their cross-country trip, a white mob in Montgomery, Alabama set their bus on fire. Attorney General Robert Kennedy was forced to send in federal marshals to protect a church meeting there when it was surrounded by a violent white mob. Blacks didn't back down, the Freedom Rides continued, and the Civil Rights Movement kept a steady pace.

On December 27, 1961, the NAACP went to court seeking the removal of a 1956 ban against its activities in Alabama. The circuit judge not only declined their request but issued a permanent injunction barring the NAACP from operating in Alabama.

The following day the Birmingham community voted to close the city recreation facilities rather than integrate the sixty-seven parks, thirty-eight playgrounds, and four golf courses. A biracial committee of citizens was formed to prevent the closings. Violence continued despite the seemingly advanced steps occurring on behalf of integration.

In October 1962 James Meredith became the first black student to enroll at the University of Mississippi. Violence and riots in response to his acceptance caused President Kennedy to send five thousand federal troops to bring peace.

Although the Rices were not victims of personal attacks like many of their friends, they could feel the heat of racism from the brutal attacks against friends in nearby neighborhoods. Several times Condi and her family carried food and clothing to family friends whose home had been bombed after relocating to a predominantly white area.

"Those terrible events burned into my consciousness," Condi recalls. "I missed many days at my segregated school because of the frequent bomb threats. Some solace to me was the piano and what a world of joy it brought me."[10]

Parents concerned for their children's lives kept them home from school, and many parents criticized those who were protesting because of the danger that put them and their families in. During the 1963 demonstrations, Condi says, she missed thirty-one days of school.

"I am so grateful to my parents for helping me through that period," says Condi. "They explained to me carefully what was going on, and they did so without any bitterness."[11]

John believed that the Civil Rights Movement needed more than external pressure. It needed internal leaders who would be willing to mentor the young, black youth of America so they would push themselves to break out of the mold that whites so willingly gave them. He knew that if he was able to help them catch the vision of education, they could rise above the white man's standards, and even above racism to a degree.

On the civil rights home front, Martin Luther King, Jr. was arrested and jailed during anti-segregation protests in Birmingham. While incarcerated, he wrote his now famous "Letter from Birmingham Jail," arguing that individuals have the moral duty to disobey unjust laws. Condi was moved by the historic letter from her hometown jail in Birmingham.

Upon King's release from jail, he petitioned President John F. Kennedy to send the National Guard to Birmingham to help get the violence against blacks under control. Bombs were continually going off in Birmingham. One devastated the home of the Rices' friend Arthur Shores, a prominent black lawyer for civil rights causes. A firebomb was tossed in Titusville, a suburb of Birmingham where Condi had been born, but it didn't go off. John went to Birmingham Police Headquarters and demanded that an investigation be made, yet none ever was. King warned President Kennedy that something horrible was going to happen if he didn't intervene.

Remembering these days, Condi refers to these attacks on

blacks as "homegrown terrorism." It was indeed a time of terror for Condi, who began to see just how far racist whites would go to destroy the black race.

"The entire black community was determined on one thing," Rice said. "It was that as America emerged from the old ways of intolerance and prejudice, the children would be ready to take their rightful place in American society."[12] Condi's parents found ways to keep life as normal as possible for her within their home despite the external chaos due to the Civil Rights Movement. During the 1962 boycott of downtown Birmingham, Condi remembers a specific example. "My parents got my toys that year from my grandmother and aunt who lived in Virginia. They had them sent to us rather than buy in the stores downtown."[13]

About the same time, when Condi was eight, Angelena orchestrated Condi's being able to begin taking weekly French lessons.

Because Condi had no siblings to play with, the piano became her best friend. Condi played for hours, and as the years went by she developed a touch of sweetness in her technique and style, just as the meaning of her name suggests. As a result she won several music competitions. Condi also became close to her schoolteachers, who were an influential aspect of her and her friends' success in school. Along with extended members of the family, all cared for and invested in the children. Underpaid teachers who had old curricula pitched in their own money to buy up-to-date school books for the kids. John and Angelena had even bought books for an entire class one year so they would be taught the same advanced curriculum as the white kids on the other side of the tracks.

John and Angelena wanted to teach Condoleezza responsibility in the area of leadership. In doing so, they implemented a family "organization" among the three of them. In this "organization," Condi was the president, Angelena was the secretary, and John was the treasurer. Whatever decision concerned them as a family or Condi, they voted, with Condi's vote carrying the most weight. They voted on where they'd go on vacation, what movie they'd see (her favorite childhood movie was *My Fair Lady*), what they'd have for dinner, or what they'd do together on a specific day. In making Condi president of the Rice home, her parents knew they were teaching their daughter to make decisions with the understanding that her choice would affect other people. Further, it would teach her how to lead a meeting and how to work with others in such an environment. Their strategy worked, although John often complained about being outvoted on topics of discussion because Angelena always favored Condi.

"She was always very secure," says Condi's maternal aunt, Geona McPhatter, laughing. "The family made all the decisions together, even as to what to have for dinner or whether to go to a segregated movie or concert. I think Condi was the firm one." [14]

In August 1963 Dr. King spoke to over two hundred thousand people, blacks and whites alike who joined him for the March on Washington. King spoke to the crowd from the Lincoln Memorial and delivered the moving speech, "I Have a Dream."

Although many churches became refuges for blacks to meet and plan strategy against segregation, one church in particular became of great interest to both blacks and the people who desired to destroy them—the 16th Street Baptist Church. Founded in 1873, it was the oldest black church in Birmingham. It was several years after 16th Street Baptist Church's birth that black Methodist churches originated in the Birmingham area, followed by the Catholic, Presbyterian, Episcopalian, Congregational, Lutheran, and Advent churches. It wasn't until after World War II that the Pentecostal Church began there.

Due to 16th Street's prominence in the black community and its central location to downtown Birmingham, the church served as headquarters for civil rights mass meetings and rallies in the early 1960s. During this time of trial, turmoil, and confrontation, the church provided strength and safety for black men, women, and children dedicated to breaking the bonds of segregation in Birmingham.

The mass meetings held in the 16th Street Baptist Church and in many other churches in Birmingham in May 1963 resulted in marches and demonstrations that produced police retaliation and brutality, still painful to the memory of all who lived in the city and millions who saw it reported on national TV newscasts.

Reverend John Cross, pastor of the 16th Street Baptist church during the late fifties and sixties, reports that they received multiple bomb threats. After the threats were made, he assigned various church members to security duty throughout the night hours, but there was no attack. Cross describes those days as having "an uneasy calm—although we were sitting on a keg of dynamite." Although his words would prove to be prophetic in nature, there was no physical evidence to support his uneasy feelings. Thinking it was just a scare tactic, the church leadership ceased to provide security—a decision they'd greatly regret in the weeks to follow. After the church leadership called off the twenty-four-hour surveillance of the church, five men began digging a small tunnel under a set of external stairs that were located on the northeast corner of the building where congregation members who attended Sunday school or got to church early entered.

It was a sunny but hazy morning on September 15, 1963. Condoleezza was eight years old and felt secure praising God in her father's church, only a few blocks away from 16th Street Baptist Church. It was Youth Day at the Baptist church, and adult members were planning to teach the children a lesson called "A Love That Forgives." As the eight or so adults concluded their preparation for the lesson, approximately eighty kids transitioned from Sunday school to the worship service. Four of those kids, little girls ranging in age between eleven and fourteen, stopped by a room at the back of the church to change into their choir robes. Suddenly at 10:22 A.M. there was a loud explosion. J. S. Goodson, a member of the church and a witness of the bombing, described the sudden explosion of dynamite as sounding like "a cannon." The explosion was so huge that it raised up the stairs to the church's back entrance where the Sunday school members had entered earlier that morning and killed Addie Mae Collins, Carole Robertson, Cynthia Wesley, and Denise McNair, the four little girls changing into their choir robes.

At the time of the bombing, Condi heard the explosion and felt the ground shaking beneath her feet two blocks away as she sang praise songs to the Lord. "It is a sound that I can still hear today," she says.[15] Everyone within earshot knew without a doubt that a bomb had gone off. The question was, where?

Pastor Cross helped everyone exit the building but soon felt the need to return to see if anyone had been harmed. He led a group of believers back into the church and found the four little girls lying on top of each other. It was a devastating day for the girls' families and the black community as a whole. Word of the deaths raced through the black community, and a blanket of mourning hovered over Birmingham. Television crews and other media circled around the church like vultures. The bombing and the deaths of the four girls made international headlines.

Along with the deaths of the four girls, twenty other members of the church were injured, and the church sustained over $300,000 worth of damages. In addition, five cars were damaged, two of them totally destroyed.

Like many churches in Birmingham, the 16th Street Baptist Church had numerous stained-glass windows that artistically framed the congregation during their worship service. One window, referred to as the Rose Window, had great significance after the bombing. It was a portrait of Jesus, staff in hand, leading children. Although the frames of most of the windows in the church and across the street from the church in a laundromat were all blown out, that one stained-glass picture of Jesus leading the children sustained no damage except in one place: the face of Jesus was blown completely out of the stained-glass portrait. Spiritual black activists saw this as a sign from above: Jesus was leading their children to liberation, and although the body of Christ could be assaulted, the body would still stand strong.

Nevertheless, the assault rattled the black community and especially its children. Condi couldn't help but take the assault personally, knowing that it could have been her. "It's one thing to be involved with marches," she said. "It's quite another to be sitting in Sunday school learning about Jesus and getting killed."

Condi and her parents attended the funeral for the four girls, which left a lasting impression. "I remember more than anything the coffins," she said. "The small coffins. And a sense that Birmingham wasn't a very safe place."[16]

Condi had been friends with two of the victims—Denise McNair, who had attended various activities with Condi, and Cynthia Wesley, who was her neighbor. "I remember being very sad about these little girls, but I don't remember having a permanent sense of fear. My parents were pretty good at giving the impression that they could protect me, even if they couldn't."[17]

Even then Condi could see what the terrorists assaulting the black community were trying to do. Remembering the day of the assault, she said, "They tried to suck hope out of the future by showing that hope could be killed—child by child."[18]

Martin Luther King, Jr. was appalled at the random attack and the killing of the girls, referring to them as "unoffending, innocent, and beautiful." There was no way their deaths could be justified. King called President Kennedy at his vacation home in the Hamptons, demanding that he intervene. This time the President responded.

The National Guard was sent to Birmingham to help bring peace to a city spinning out of control from hatred. National Guardsmen brought some stability but were often accused of purposefully turning away from some acts of violence and allowing some prejudices to remain.

Fifty-nine-year-old Robert Edward Chambliss, also known as "Dynamite Bob," was a husband, father, and mechanic for a Birmingham garage and was suspected of being the ringleader and a participant in the bombing with friend and conspirator Bobby

Frank Cherry. Chambliss was a former Ku Klux Klan member who had been convicted of beating a black man in the forties for no apparent reason. He was questioned by both local police and the FBI, then was charged and acquitted for possessing dynamite. The apparent disregard and prejudice toward the black girls' lives enraged black advocates and demonstrators, and more riots broke out in Birmingham.

Chambliss would be tried for the murder of the youngest victim, Denise McNair, fourteen years later. But the FBI "lost" the files and physical evidence on Chambliss, and the prosecutor was forced to use personal testimony. Surprisingly, the most damaging testimony came from within Chambliss's own home. Elizabeth Cobb, an ordained minister and Chambliss's niece, testified that he had told her "he had enough stuff to put away, to flatten half of Birmingham," and "You just wait until after Sunday morning, and they will beg us to let them segregate." Cobb described her uncle as a volatile man who despised blacks and attempts at integration. Further testimony from a friend of Chambliss's wife revealed that Mrs. Chambliss had walked into a room of their house and saw her husband with four large bundles "of what looked like large firecrackers." The prosecuting documents showed that Chambliss had planted nineteen sticks of dynamite. On the basis of those damaging testimonies, the three black and nine white jury members convicted Chambliss and sentenced him to life in prison.

Four other men were sought in the bombing. One took everything he knew to his deathbed, two others made deathbed confessions, and Thomas Blanton, Jr. would eventually be convicted and also sentenced to life in prison for helping Chambliss in the bombing.

Martin Luther King, Jr.'s work and leadership in the Civil Rights Movement earned him *Time's* 1963 Man of the Year Award. As a result, the movement was given even more of a push, and after reading about his many accomplishments on behalf of the black race, more and more whites began to advocate for the war-torn race.

The Civil Rights Act was finally brought before Congress on June 11, 1963. President Kennedy pointed out, "The Negro baby born in America today, regardless of the section of the nation in which he is born, has about one-half as much chance of completing high school as a white baby born in the same place on the same day; one third as much chance of completing college; one third as much chance of becoming a professional man; twice as much chance of becoming unemployed; about one-seventh as much chance of earning $10,000 a year; a life expectancy which is seven years shorter; and the prospects of earning only half as much."[19]

Only two months later, on November 22, eight days after Condi's ninth birthday, President John F. Kennedy, barely beyond his first thousand days in office, was killed by Lee Harvey Oswald as his motorcade wound through Dallas, Texas. Oswald claimed that he was a patsy and denied the charges. Two days later Oswald was shot and killed by Jack Ruby on live television while in police custody. President Kennedy's Civil Rights Act was still being debated by Congress when he died.

During that same year Condi and her parents had taken their summer vacation to Washington, D.C., where they visited the White House. As she stood outside the gate before that large building, she told her parents that someday she'd be inside—and she didn't mean just to visit.

THE PRE-TEEN YEARS

When Condi was ten, she got tired of all the piano lessons and felt overwhelmed with the pressure that practicing put on her. She had been dedicated to the piano for seven years, often staying up until 2:30 or 3 in the morning to practice, and it was getting old.

"I got really bored with the piano and wanted to quit," Condi remembers. "It's the only time my parents ever intervened. My mother said, 'You're not old enough or good enough to make that decision. When you are old enough and good enough, then you can quit, but not now.'"

Looking back, Condi's glad she didn't quit, but the pressure her parents put on her to be better and different than others was difficult at times. "It was great being my parents' daughter, but sometimes it was terrible," Condi confesses. She remembers a grade school variety show that she and her friends wanted to perform in together. The girls planned to dress up as the Supremes and do a number to wow the crowd.

"My father decided it was undignified," she says. Her parents arranged instead for her to tap dance by herself, something she'd never done. Condi wasn't thrilled with the idea. "But my parents convinced me that what I was going to do was special," Condi remembers, "and it was better to be special than part of a Supremes act."[1]

The Rices hired a dance teacher to teach Condi to tap to the song "Sweet Sue." "I had this particular outfit, and my father stood there by the stage with his arms crossed to make sure nobody laughed. That's the way my parents were. I was always supposed to do something different and special, and slightly more refined."[2]

The year 1964 started out as a good one for blacks. On January 23 the 24th Amendment abolished the poll tax, which had been originally instituted in eleven southern states after Reconstruction to make it difficult for poor blacks to vote. The abolishment of the poll tax brought hope to blacks, and they jumped at the opportunity to exercise their new right.

In the summer of 1964 a campaign was launched in the United States called Freedom Summer. Several organizations collaborated their efforts to register as many black voters as possible in the southern states. Over a thousand volunteers came together to accomplish their task, aimed particularly at Mississippi, where the African-American population exceeded 45 percent but only 5 percent voted. As a result more than sixteen hundred blacks became eligible to vote. The program also established many summer school programs in Mississippi to counteract the state's inequitably funded school system and sent delegates to the Democratic National Convention to protest the official all-white Mississippi contingent.

While Freedom Summer brought change, it also brought heartache. Violence quickly assaulted the campaign. On June 21 three youth—James Chaney, a black Mississippian, and Michael Schwerner and Andrew Goodman, two northern white volunteers—were abducted and killed. Their bodies were found later in an earthen dam. While seven men would be eventually convicted for the civil rights deaths, it would take over forty years for justice to be carried out fully.

Vice President Lyndon Baines Johnson had stepped up to be President of the United States after John F. Kennedy's unexpected death, and blacks were concerned. Historically President Johnson had a poor record on civil rights issues. But Johnson pleasantly surprised civil rights advocates and took up the cause even though that offended many of his friends and colleagues who quickly became his adversaries. His main opponent was his longtime friend and mentor Richard B. Russell, who told the Senate, "We will resist to the bitter end any measure or any movement which would have a tendency to bring about social equality and intermingling and amalgamation of the races in our [Southern] states." Russell received support from eighteen Southern Democratic senators to help abolish the Civil Rights Act.

But in a private meeting on June 15, 1964 Russell told two leading supporters of the Civil Rights Act, Mike Mansfield and Hubert Humphrey, that he would end his fight against the bill, and when the vote was taken, it passed by 73 votes to 27.[3] The passing of the Civil Rights Act would enforce the constitutional right for minorities to vote, bring relief against discrimination in public facilities and public education, prevent discrimination in federally assisted programs, and establish a Commission on Equal Employment Opportunity. It was a hard-won victory for the African-American race and their sympathizers.

The changes occurred slowly in other establishments. Only days after the Civil Rights Act was passed, the Rices decided to blatantly test the waters by going to eat at an all-white restaurant. "The people there stopped eating for a couple of minutes," remembers Condi. No one said anything, but then the crowd stopped staring and began eating again.[4] "A few weeks later we went through a drive-in," Condi says, "and when we drove away I bit into my hamburger—and it was all onions."[5]

Shortly after the Civil Rights Act was passed, Dr. King received the Nobel Peace Prize and $54,123 in prize money. Generous in heart, he gave the money to charities and organizations working to gain equal rights for African-Americans. At the age of thirty-five King was the youngest man to have ever received the coveted prize.

America began to take further notice, and he was awarded five honorary degrees from various institutions.

During these years Condi temporarily let go of her dream to be a concert pianist but still practiced with determination, and her parents allowed her to explore other aspects of music as well. Condi learned to play the flute and violin, and she pursued dance and ballet classes with a renewed passion. She also began taking her ice-skating more seriously.

In the summer of 1964, at nearly ten years of age, Condi was invited to attend the all-white, newly-integrated Birmingham Southern Conservatory of Music to study piano, where she began to compete professionally, winning many honors. She was the first black person to enroll in that prestigious conservatory. In the meantime she was so far advanced academically that she was able to skip the seventh grade entirely.

The following year, 1965, John was offered and accepted a position as Dean of Students at Stillman College in Tuscaloosa, Alabama, fifty-eight miles from Birmingham. Stillman College was where John's father had attended college, so it had a special place in his heart. He jumped at the opportunity.

The Rices moved to Tuscaloosa, and after getting settled in, John looked for ways to begin mentoring young minds again in his new environment. He became chairman of the advisory board of Project Head Start and a member of the board of directors for the Tuscaloosa Opportunity Program. He also stayed active in the lives of his previous congregation at Westminster through phone calls and occasional visits when he was in town visiting family.

"Even after they moved to Tuscaloosa, not a month would pass that Reverend Rice didn't call me," remembers Annye Marie Downing. "Anything I had a problem with, I knew I could call on him. At one point I became a little despondent with the church after they left, and I stopped going. I'd call him and talk to him about it. He said, 'Get some books and read about your faith.' He'd tell me not to stay out of church. I was dependent on him spiritually. John was a fun guy. Sometimes to cheer me up he'd call and change his voice and ask for me, but I always knew who it was."

Condi bloomed wherever she was planted, and although she had to leave the Southern Conservatory of Music when they moved to Tuscaloosa, she practiced with discipline and looked for opportunities to perform and compete, again grasping hold of the goal of being a concert pianist.

Along with piano, Condi continued to grow spiritually. She'd spend hours debating and talking about the Bible with her father, who happily obliged his daughter's conversations.

During the following year Condi was spiritually confronted (as were many readers) by a *Time* magazine cover that boldly asked, "Is God Dead?" The article that supported the cover was called "Toward a Hidden God." The writer wrote the article as a summons to reflect on the meaning of existence in a broad attempt to challenge both people of faith and atheists. The article became a fiercely debated issue in American theology. Scholarly religious journals were overflowing with rebuttals, and pulpits around the world rang with rebuke that anyone would ever consider such an idea.

The article served to *confirm* Condi's faith, not weaken it. "I can honestly say, without exaggeration, that not a single day of my life have I doubted the existence of God. . . . For me, that was never a question, especially in my home."[6] For the budding teen it was never even considered an option.

At age twelve, Condi learned something that would be embedded in her heart for the rest of her life. During a visit to her grandmother's house, her Uncle Alto, the one on whom she'd had a girlish crush, became deathly ill. While her parents and other relatives rushed about the house frantically trying to get him to the hospital, Condi's Grandma Ray sat quietly on her bed with her arms folded. Seeing the contrast between the rest of her family and her grandmother, Condi asked, "Grandmother, aren't you worried about Alto?" In response her grandmother answered, "God's will be done."

"That was it: four simple but profound words," remembers Condi. "Those words struck a chord in my heart that has resonated ever since. How many of us say that without meaning it? We repeat it again and again in the Lord's Prayer, but we don't walk in it, becoming chaotic when difficult circumstances arise."

Seeing her grandmother's quiet spirit convinced her that God was in control in the midst of crisis, and that would prove to be a foundational core belief for Condi during the turbulent years that she would have to endure and overcome as an adult.

On March 7, 1965 blacks began a march from Selma to Montgomery, Alabama in support of voting rights but were stopped along the way by a police blockade. The officers used tear gas, whips, and clubs against the marchers on what the media would call Bloody Sunday. Fifty marchers were hospitalized.

On August 6, 1965 the Voting Rights Act was signed into law by President Lyndon Johnson. The Act would outlaw the requirement that would-be voters in the United States take literacy tests or pay a poll tax to qualify to register to vote. It also provided for federal registration of voters instead of state or local voter registration, which had often been denied to minorities and poor voters. The act also provided for Department of Justice oversight to voter registration and the Department's approval for any change in voting law in districts whose populations were at least 5 percent black. It is said that the events that occurred on Bloody Sunday gave blacks the anger to push the Act through the legal system.

On a roll, President Johnson asserted that civil rights laws alone were not enough to remedy discrimination. So on September 24 he issued Executive Order 11246, which enforced affirmative action for the first time. It required government contractors to "take affirmative action" toward prospective minority employees in all aspects of hiring and employment.

Despite the changes that were occurring on behalf of blacks, some felt the need to fight back. So in October 1966 the militant Black Panthers were founded by Huey Newton and Bobby Seale in

Oakland, California. Originally espousing violent revolution as the only means of achieving black liberation, the Black Panthers called on African-Americans to arm themselves for the liberation struggle. Hundreds of blacks joined the party and became involved in multiple violent confrontations with police, resulting in several deaths. Eventually the party would split, and one faction announced its intention of abandoning violent methods to gain liberation.

The Transformation of a Woman-Child

*J*ohn was at Stillman College less than two years when he applied for and received an offer to be the assistant dean at the College of Arts and Sciences and assistant director of admissions at the University of Denver. He knew that taking Condi to a more metropolitan area would provide more diversity in extracurricular activities and opportunity for a better education. John was also worried about the bombings that were becoming more and more frequent in the South. Additionally, it would give both him and Angelena the opportunity to get their Master's degrees at the university. The family had loved visiting Denver on summer vacations; so after they voted as a family on making the move, the Rices packed up and left Tuscaloosa in the summer of 1967.

The Rices found an apartment building to rent temporarily while John got settled at the university. Angelena began teaching at a small private school across town. Eventually they would move into an integrated, middle-class area of Denver on a busy street not far from the university and from the school Condi attended.

John and Angelena enrolled Condi in the prestigious St. Mary's Academy located in Englewood, a suburb of Denver. For the first time in Condoleezza's life, she would attend an integrated school, although she'd be only one of three blacks enrolled there. St. Mary's Academy was an independent, Catholic school founded in 1964 by the Catholic Sisters of Loretto, and while it boasts of a legacy of pioneering, risk-taking, and service to others, only 21 percent of their students have ever been of color.

Although she was definitely part of a minority at St. Mary's, the experience didn't affect her negatively, as she was neither intimidated nor uncomfortable with the racial odds. What she does remember is that she had to wear a uniform for the first time, which, she says, was overshadowed by the joy of being able to ice-skate year-round in Denver's covered ice-skating rinks.

Since Alabama was segregated (if not legally, at least socially), Condi and her parents had been concerned that the education she had received in the Birmingham School District wouldn't be as good as that in predominantly white schools in Denver. Their worries were needless. After enrolling Condi in St. Mary's Academy, they all realized that the education she'd received in segregated, less-desirable schools on the black side of Birmingham was as good as it was in schools on the white side of town. The extra effort of the underpaid black teachers who bought schoolbooks for the children and were dedicated to tutoring students on their own time had paid off. Condi was able to pick up at St. Mary's where she'd left off in Alabama.

Around the same time that the Rices moved to Denver, Condi struggled a little bit with her identity. On one hand she had a passion for attending operas and art museums with her mother and adamantly desired to be a concert pianist. On the other hand she was very athletic and loved watching football games on television with her father, memorizing plays, athletes' names, and positions. Condi struggled with how the two loves—opera and football—on the opposite ends of the spectrum could live within the same person. She received peace when she came to the understanding that was simply the way God had made her, and she began to relish the diversity within her.

Dr. Martin Luther King continued to travel and spoke virtually anywhere he was asked to do so. In the eleven-year period between 1957 and 1968 he traveled over six million miles and spoke over twenty-five hundred times. While on the road speaking, he wrote five books and was a featured contributor to many magazines and newspapers. As a result of his open defiance against racism, he was arrested more than twenty times and was assaulted numerous times.

On the evening of April 4, 1968, while standing on the balcony of his motel room in Memphis, Tennessee, where he was to lead a protest march in sympathy with striking garbage workers of that city, King was assassinated by James Earl Ray, an escaped convict who had broken out of the Missouri State Penitentiary a year before. King's death set off riots in 125 U.S. cities. Ray would later be captured and sentenced to ninety-nine years in prison and would publicly deny being the shooter, saying others were involved. His words have led to various conspiracy theories regarding the circumstances around King's death.

In the meantime the Civil Rights Movement continued to generate change for blacks. On April 11 President Johnson signed the Civil Rights Act of 1968, prohibiting discrimination in the sale, rental, and financing of housing.

White supremacists hoped that King's death would immobilize the black community, if not block the success of the movement in its entirety, but instead it fueled it. Twenty-four days later Dr. Ralph Abernathy succeeded King, and on May 12 Abernathy led a march on Washington called a Poor People's March. A campsite was erected on the Capitol grounds called Resurrection City, aimed at bringing legislators' attention to the plight of America's poor, who were predominantly African-American. Black America was not giving up.

In 1967 President Johnson had appointed the first black United

States Supreme Court Justice, Thurgood Marshall, who as a child was punished for misbehaving in school by being forced to read the Constitution, which he later said heightened an interest in that document. Marshall was the grandson of a slave and would serve to be instrumental in the Civil Rights Movement in the judicial realm. He would eventually go on to be a top aide to President Bill Clinton.

In 1968 Democrat Shirley Chisholm was elected to be the first African-American United States Congresswoman for New York's 12th District and would serve for seven terms. Four years before being elected to Congress, Chisholm had successfully run for the New York State Legislature. Chisholm would also be the first African-American and the first woman to make a serious bid to be President of the United States in 1972.

On November 21, 1969 John Rice proposed that the University of Denver hold a Black Studies Seminar entitled "The Black Experience in America." It would involve a class lecture and an open forum and provide the opportunity for individual students to meet informally with the guest speakers. John sought to "develop rapport and relate positively with people of varying racial and social backgrounds so that social issues and problems may be clearly explained, discussed and understood by them without prejudice."[1]

John initiated the "Black Experience in America" seminar to bring a real knowledge of the black man and his problems to the university community. Despite the fact that Condi was still only in high school, John and Angelena brought Condi to the seminars to help educate her and give solidity to her faith and her heritage as part of the black race.

The University of Denver was shocked when more than 150 students signed up for John's class, and it only grew as it was advertised on campus through the university publications and in the Denver newspapers. Heavy hitters of the black race topped the list of names coming to speak at the university as John had many friends on the high end of the civil rights ladder: Charles G. Hurst, Jr. president of Malcolm X College in Chicago; U.S. track medalist Lee Evans, and also John Carlos, who was involved in the black power controversy during the 1968 Olympic Games in Mexico City; former U.S. Ambassador to Ghana Franklin H. Williams; members of the U.S. Commission on Civil Rights; comedian and civil rights leader Dick Gregory; Arvarh E. Strickland, historian; Dr. David Abernathy; Eugene Perkins, poet and playwright; and Georgia State Representative Julian Bond.

Among John's civil rights speakers was a woman by the name of Fannie Lou Hamer, a Mississippi sharecropper who changed the nation's perspective on democracy by becoming involved in the Civil Rights Movement. Hamer continually risked her life because of her civil rights activism, enduring brutal beatings for advocating for equal rights. Despite being a full-time mother, Hamer spoke frequently to raise money for the Civil Rights Movement and helped organize and lead the Mississippi Freedom Democratic Party to challenge the white domination of the Democratic Party.

Hamer was deeply committed to improving life for poor minorities in Mississippi and worked with the National Council of Negro Women and others, organizing food cooperatives and other services. She continued political activities as well, helping convene the National Women's Political Caucus in the 1970s. When Hamer spoke to John's class, she made quite the impression on the then fourteen-year-old Condi's heart.

"I will never forget meeting . . . Fannie Lou Hamer when I was a teenager," remembers Condi. "She came to the University of Denver to speak to my father's class. She was not sophisticated in the way we think of it, yet so compelling that I remember the power of her message even today. In 1964, Fannie Lou Hamer refused to listen to those who told her that a sharecropper with a sixth-grade education could not, or should not, launch a challenge that would dismantle the racist infrastructure of Mississippi's Democratic Party. She did it anyway. And Ms. Hamer reminds us that heroes are not born—they are made; and they often come from unlikely places."[2]

Racism and prejudice were evident in Denver, but not as blatantly as in Birmingham. John and Angelena were nonetheless shocked when a school counselor at St. Mary's Academy advised them that their daughter was not college material. "I had not done very well on the preliminary SAT exam," remembers Condi. "I remember thinking that the odd thing about it was that [the counselor] had not bothered to check my record. I was a straight-A student in all advanced courses. I was excelling in Latin. I was a figure skater and a piano student. That none of that occurred to her I think was a subtle form of racism. It was the problem of low expectation [for blacks]."[3] Appalled at the counselor's overview of Condi and her ability to obtain a college education, John and Angelena rejected the woman's biased opinion wholeheartedly and encouraged Condi to do the same. Still, the prejudiced attitude made its mark on the teen as she grappled with the counselor's lack of encouragement.

Condi continued to play music and competed at every opportunity given her. Shortly after getting to Denver she enrolled in a regional young artists' piano competition where she played Mozart's *D Minor Piano Concerto* and won. The fervent and musically stimulating piece remains a favorite of hers to this day. Other works that she is passionate about include Brahms's *B Flat Major Piano Concerto*, Brahms's *Piano Quintet*, Beethoven's *Symphony No. 7*, and Mussorgsky's *Boris Glazunov*.

Condi also became heavily involved with ice-skating, rising at 4:30 every morning and practicing before school. She entered and competed in several ice-skating competitions, winning several awards. While she didn't always take first place, she was definitely eager and was determined to place somewhere in the top three.

According to Dr. John Leslie Blackburn, professor at the University of Alabama and a friend of John's, the Rices had one focus—Condi's success. "The Rices weren't known for having a lot of money, but what they did have they willingly invested in Condi believing she'd succeed," he says, adding, "They were right."

Blackburn first met John Rice when John was the dean at Stillman College and was getting ready to move to Denver. The two men quickly developed a strong bond over discussions regarding integration. Shortly thereafter Blackburn received an offer at the University of Denver to work with John and left Alabama. He and his family moved two doors down from the Rices and spent a lot of time with them as a family at neighborhood gatherings. Blackburn's daughter, Holly, became particularly fond of Condi, who was nine years her senior, and looked up to her as a mentor. According to Blackburn, Condi tried to teach Holly piano. "I always said that Condi wanted to quit playing the piano after she tried to teach my daughter Holly how to play," Blackburn said, laughing.

Blackburn and John became even closer as they worked together at the University of Denver. Blackburn says, "When I went to the University of Denver as Vice Chancellor of Student Affairs, John was finishing his Master's Degree and was working in the College of Arts and Sciences and teaching a Black Experience course. We ended up working as a team for many years. In the seventies [in Denver], young people were really searching for religious experiences, and the church in general didn't really know how to respond to these people. As a result, they did a poor job. John was very effective in working with these people and spent a lot of time working with students who had concerns about their faith. He made no exception to the fact that he was a minister, and you could see that in just the way he talked and the way he behaved. As a result, at functions at the University the Chancellor would always call on John for prayer, and several people went to him privately for prayer."

John retained his passion for mentorship and would often have students lined up outside his office waiting to talk with him. Moses Brewer was one such student.

"He had a parade of people who would come by his office," remembers Brewer. "If you had a problem and you just needed to talk to somebody, you could go by and visit with Dean Rice at his office. He would sit with you as you shared and would take time out to talk to you, all the while there was somebody else waiting outside to do the same. He made the stay at the university a very rewarding one for me and everyone he came into contact with.

"I would go by to see him late in the afternoon, and he'd say, 'Come with me! I'm going to pick up Angie.' I'd go with him, and we'd have those fatherly types of conversations on the way to pick Angelena up from this little school where she was teaching. But he wasn't just instrumental in my life, but in the lives of many students at the university. He cared about people, and you could tell by the programs he implemented. For one, he was very, very instrumental in creating harmony and a better understanding between minority students on campus. Then he created a program called the Education Opportunity Program (EOP) for all students. If you had a financial difficulty, you could go to the EOP office and get a student loan or grant, but you didn't have to pay it back. It was an emergency grant in the range of three hundred dollars to eight hundred dollars. The money came from all the parking meters on campus. So kids who couldn't afford books for school or who didn't have money for rent or were experiencing another emergency would have a resource to go to.

"As we crept into the seventies, he was also involved with the student leaders on campus. The student leaders had a high regard for him and a respect for him because he always demonstrated an ethical character and he demonstrated commitment and listened to students' concerns. He also developed a group that addressed some of the issues with civil rights. Because of this he was instrumental in pretty much establishing communication and dialogue between the students and the administration. He was a very good listener and had the feel of a grandparent or a father figure to him.

"He was a robust kind of guy, and he enunciated and articulated his words in such a way that everyone sat up and listened. For example, across the country in 1971 there were a lot of problems with black students being shot and killed. We had some black students down in South Carolina and Mississippi and other states who were killed where demonstrations were taking place. There was a lot of tension in our city and on our campus. They were getting ready to shut the college campus down. Dean Rice was instrumental in calming the voices of students and administration. We had military on campus—the National Guard was there to keep the school open. So it didn't get to where there was a riot or anything of that nature."

John mentored Brewer for the remainder of his tenure as a student, then helped him create a job helping students who came from out of state remain active so they wouldn't get lonely and discouraged though so far away from home. It was a difficult transition for Brewer, who instantly went from being a star basketball player on campus to an administrator. As his boss, John continued to mentor Brewer, helping him in the transition, and even invited him over to his home several times and to activities with his family.

"He was like a father to me. I was very close to him. He allowed me to be a part of his world. We had a lot in common coming from the South, and we often talked about his coaching experience. He gave me a lot of constant mentoring about being an administrator because of the transition from being a basketball player on campus and everybody knows you to [being] an administrator. He'd encourage me to go back and get my Master's Degree, which I did. And he encouraged me to conduct and carry myself in none other than a professional way. He taught me not to look at the negative but to look at the positive, and I wanted to be like him."

John also mentored Brewer spiritually and continually encouraged him through example to do what was right. "His spiritual influence on me was quite remarkable," says Brewer. "His spiritual being was always tied into doing the right thing. There was a situation where we were together on a trip for the university, and there was this beautiful woman, an administrator whom we met from another school. I had a camera and took some pictures of John and the woman, and there were some pictures of me and the woman. Later on at our hotel room he asked for the pictures, so I gave them to him. He tore them up, and as he did he said, 'It's not that I don't trust you, Mo—I just don't want to give people the wrong impression.' I just thought it was incredible that he wanted to protect his integrity in that way."

Little by little Brewer became an extended part of the Rice family, spending time with the Rices, watching football and attending performance events where Condi played the piano and athletic competitions in which she was competing.

"Condi was not the typical young person," Brewer remembers. "She was, as we say down in the South, an 'old soul.' In other words, she was very mature for her age. She didn't play like other girls her age. She was focused on being a concert pianist. She was always playing in a recital or competing at skating, and I would go with Dean Rice and Angelena to see her perform. I was a grown man, and she was playing different recital pieces that I hadn't ever heard of myself. But I would go and listen to her play that wonderful music.

"Condi was a debutante at the University of Denver. The debutante program was a group of young, African-American ladies whom we would 'present' to the community. These were young ladies who excelled in academics and were also involved in community types of volunteerism."

During his frequent trips to the Rice home, Brewer got to know Condi personally including her likes and dislikes.

"Condi loved football. She loved the Cincinnati Bengals and would talk about them endlessly. Isaac Curtis was one of her favorite players at the time. She was so big on football that she knew everything. She knew all the drafts and who was drafting who and was very educated in the sports arena.

"Whenever I saw Condi we'd talk about football. All our interaction was tied into sports. When I would be over at her house she was talking about the draft choices. She'd say, 'Why was this team picking this guy up?' And so she would always be with Dean Rice and me talking about football."

For many years John's health had been a concern for him and his family. He was overweight, suffered with diabetes, and had high blood pressure, extreme gout, heart problems, and various other illnesses. He took several medications to ease his pain but often suffered from the side effects associated with them. Despite his many illnesses, he seldom missed work and stayed focused on his family and their needs rather than his own. He knew that his health might lead to a premature death and asked Brewer to take care of his girls if something should happen to him. Brewer committed to do what he could in the event that he should pass prematurely. John also talked endlessly about Angelena and Condi, telling Brewer and anyone else who would listen how much they meant to him. Brewer says that the relationship between John, Angelena, and Condi was unique and unable to be penetrated by outsiders.

"They had this veil around them, and they wouldn't let anyone else in. Even though I spent time with them, they still had their own togetherness. They didn't let anybody come into that inner circle of their world. Even just John and Angelena had a unique relationship as a married couple. They were soul mates and did everything together. He didn't go anyplace without her and only went to events where she could go. She was at all his Black Experience classes, and they had something very important in common: Condi."

The following year John began to conduct fall classes on the history of Africa up to 1800 at the University of Denver. He wanted to show both whites and blacks the rich African-American heritage, and he wanted opportunities to reach larger groups of students. His main objective was to teach students the truth about the history of African-Americans—where they originated and how they persevered throughout extreme oppression and slavery for hundreds of years.

About that same time Angelena joined the university's administrative staff and also began attending classes to get her Master's degree with John.

Condi became even more serious about her education and received honors at St. Mary's. Every minute of every waking hour she was honing her ice-skating or musical talent or was in school or studying.

During Condi's junior year of high school at St. Mary's, John and Angelena encouraged her to graduate early and go directly to college at the University of Denver. Condi, however, felt strongly about graduating with her new friends. In a compromise, Condi agreed to take classes at the University of Denver's Lamont School of Music while finishing her senior year at St. Mary's. As a gift her parents bought her a $13,000 Steinway piano for her to use as she studied music at the university.

Getting up every morning at 4:30 A.M., Condi would practice her ice-skating, take two classes at the university pursuing a degree in piano performance, and attend St. Mary's in the afternoon. During the evening she would do her homework from both schools and practice piano, sometimes until late into the morning hours.

One morning as sixteen-year-old Condi sat in a lecture hall at the University of Denver, one of three blacks out of approximately 250 students, something occurred that challenged the very essence of who she was as an individual. A professor began approvingly citing William Shockley.

Shockley was notorious for two things—his invention of the transistor in 1947 and his disregard for the black race. After studying electronics for twenty years, in 1963 Shockley became interested in the origins of human intelligence. Although he had no formal training in genetics or psychology, he began to formulate a theory of what he called dysgenics. Using data from the U.S. Army's crude pre-induction IQ tests, he concluded that African-Americans were inherently less intelligent than Caucasians.

Shockley pursued his inflammatory ideas in a series of articles and speeches throughout the world and convinced many people that what he was proclaiming was fact. Still others met his theories with great opposition. The *Atlanta Constitution* compared his theories to Nazi genetic experiments. Shockley argued that remedial educational programs were a waste of time. He suggested that individuals with IQs below 100 be paid to undergo voluntary sterilization. He donated openly and repeatedly to a so-called Nobel sperm bank designed to pass on the genes of geniuses.

As the professor at the University of Denver quoted Shockley's theories that blacks had lower IQs because of genetics, Condi became more and more furious. "I raised my hand and said, 'You really should not be presenting this as fact because there's plenty of evidence to the contrary.'" The professor disagreed with her, saying that evidence to the contrary didn't exist. "That's when I said, 'Let me explain to you: I speak French, I play Bach, I'm better in your culture than you are. So obviously this can be taught. It doesn't have anything to do with whether you are or are not black.'"[4]

Her confrontation silenced the professor on the topic, and she even aced the class.

Shortly after Condi began taking classes at the University of Denver, Angelena found a lump in one of her breasts. The doctors recommended surgery to find out if it was benign or cancer—it was the latter.

"When I found out that my mother first had cancer . . . I found myself asking an endless amount of questions that, for the first time in my life, no one had pat answers for," remembers Condi. "My father told me that when the results of my mother's first surgery came back, he got down on his knees and prayed, 'Lord, how am I going to raise a fifteen-year-old girl alone?'"[5]

The news of Angelena's cancer was devastating for the family as Angelena's fragile humanity was challenged. She was a petite woman, and they all wondered how cancer and its treatment would affect her. For Condi, her mother's illness challenged her intellect as she realized that no amount of knowledge could help her overcome the fear of her mother's pending sickness and the probability of her death. The rubber hit the proverbial spiritual road in Condi's life, and she was forced to cling to God in a way she never had before.

"During those years, I feared her [my mother's] death in the abstract every waking day. People who have cancer, and families who live in the shadow of terminal illness, clearly understand my fear. I could not fathom how I would survive her death. I tried to imagine life without her. What was I going to do? What would replace our nightly [conversations]? How could I ever survive Christmas or a birthday without my mother there? No intellect could soothe the hurt that was there. . . . My father and I prayed that she might live to see me grow up."[6]

As her mother began treatment at a local hospital, the Lord answered John and Condi's prayers. Angelena got better, and the Rices became even more committed to appreciating life together.

After Angelena's cancer began to be treated, John was offered and accepted the position of assistant director of admissions at the University of Denver. This new position gave him the responsibility to increase student enrollment at the university as a whole. The university didn't have a problem attracting white students, but they needed more minority students. John jumped on his new role with renewed passion.

Holding back no punches, John boldly told his supervisors and colleagues that the University of Denver needed to step up to the plate when it came to advocating for and enrolling minorities. He felt that it was a national problem and one for which the university should pioneer a solution. Some of the interventions John advocated for and implemented included enlarging a program with high schools to bring disadvantaged seniors there to take studies to go toward their college education as Condi had done, as well as expanding their scholarship programs. Rice knew he was on the right track. He'd been mentoring and working with youth all of his career and knew how to reach them.

John recognized that there was great difficulty involved in creating an awareness of social problems at the university. He boldly told the faculty, "We had to have a fire in Chicago before people realized ghettos existed there; we had to have a march on Washington before people realized discrimination existed in the U.S. This should not be necessary. We should do it out of an awareness of the needs of

Westminster Presbyterian Church, 1950s era. Founded and pastored by Condoleezza's paternal grandfather, John Wesley I, then pastored by her father. Condoleezza and her parents lived in a small four-room apartment built into the back of the church. *Birmingham Public Library Archives. Used with permission.*

1955—Angelena, Condoleezza, and John Rice on a Sunday morning on the steps of Westminster Presbyterian Church that John Wesley Rice, Sr. founded and Condoleezza's father pastored. *Rice Family Photo Album.*

The parsonage that members of Westminster had built for Condoleezza and her parents shortly after her second birthday. *Birmingham Public Library Archives. Used with permission.*

Christmas 1957—Condi's suspicion of Santa is, she says, because he's the first white person she remembers seeing. *Rice Family Photo Album.*

A young John Wesley Rice II, the pastor of Westminster Presbyterian Church. *Rice Family Photo Album.*

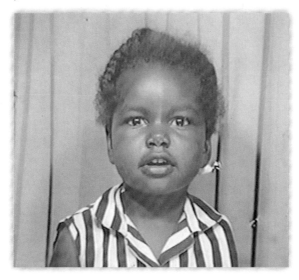

1958—A four-year-old Condi looks bright-eyed at the photographer. *Rice Family Photo Album.*

1958—The serious looking five-year-old was focused from early on. *Rice Family Photo Album.*

A snowy morning in Birmingham, Alabama, where Condi was raised. This day she made snowballs and played with her multi-racial dolls. *Rice Family Photo Album.*

Nine-year-old Condoleezza outside the White House. It was this day that she told her parents that one day she'd be inside that house. *Rice Family Photo Album.*

1967—Angelena, Condoleezza, and John Rice at Westminster Presbyterian Church. *Rice Family Photo Album.*

Condoleezza learned to play the piano at three years of age. As she matured she desired to be a concert pianist. *Rice Family Photo Album.*

Condoleezza competed semi-professionally as a skater. She was always focused, rising at 4:30 in the morning to practice. *Rice Family Photo Album.*

Angelena observes her daughter playing a hymn. *Rice Family Photo Album.*

A rare Rice family photo shortly after moving to Denver. While it was not unusual to find photos of Angelena and Condi smiling, John usually has a solemn look. *Rice Family Photo Album.*

Condoleezza with an unknown boy at her high school prom. He was a college student at the University of Denver where she also attended part-time. *Rice Family Photo Album.*

Condoleezza's first year of college at the University of Denver. She was fifteen years old. *Rice Family Photo Album.*

John Rice and his two favorite "girls," Condoleezza and Angelena. *Rice Family Photo Album.*

Pretty in pink, a twenty-year-old Condi played a piano concert at Westminster Presbyterian Church. *Rice Family Photo Album.*

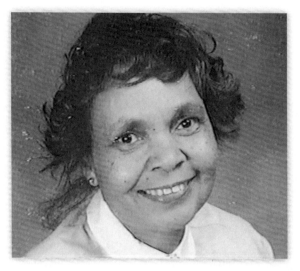

A radiant Angelena Rice, in 1983—two years before her death of breast cancer. *Rice Family Photo Album.*

1988—Condoleezza, her father John, and her stepmother, Clara Bailey-Rice on John and Clara's wedding day. Condi served as the Maid of Honor. *Rice Family Photo Album.*

John Wesley Rice, Jr. *University of Denver Special Collections & Archives. Used with permission.*

Professor Condoleezza Rice at Stanford University. *Stanford University News Service Library. Used with permission.*

Condoleezza with students at The Center for a New Generation, an afterschool program for gifted students that she founded with her father, stepmother, and philanthropist Susan Ford. *Rice Family Photo Album.*

After becoming provost, Condi's father and stepmother, Clara, encouraged her to upgrade her wheels from the beat-up Buick she'd named Boris and had driven for years. In doing so, she bought a Mercedes. *Rice Family Photo Album.*

An ailing John Rice and Condi after his first attack of arrhythmia in the spring of 2000. *Rice Family Photo Album.*

Advisor for then President George Bush, Condoleezza and Brent Scowcroft share national defense strategy. *Rice Family Photo Album.*

1992—Condoleezza, Barbara, then President George Bush, and John Rice. *Rice Family Photo Album.*

our fellow man. Education must change to teach minorities. Only one-fifth of all eligible blacks go to college."

In April 1971 the Supreme Court (in *Swann v. Charlotte-Mecklenburg Board of Education*) implemented busing as a legitimate means for achieving integration of public schools. The Court stated that because bus transportation had traditionally been contracted by school systems, busing could be used to correct racial imbalances. The order was largely unwelcome and sometimes violently opposed in local school districts but would be implemented and remain in effect until the late 1990s.

The following year Condi graduated from St. Mary's Academy with honors, received an honors scholarship from the University of Denver, and began attending as a full-time student. This was life-changing for her. Both she and her parents worked hard on their education (John and Angelena both received their Master's degree in less than two years).

Condi began writing for the university newspaper, served as a justice in the student government, taught piano, and served as chairman of student campus presentations. When asked why she worked so hard and was involved in so many things, she explained that when you are black and female, you have to work twice as hard as everyone else—words she'd heard since she was a baby.

Alongside her parents, Condi was also active in church. "When I was a college student at the University of Denver I was singing with the Montview Boulevard Presbyterian church choir, a large 80-voice, semi-professional choir."[7]

It was there that she learned and fell in love with the hardly known, rarely played Beethoven piece *Christ on the Mount of Olives*. It is a piece that later in his life Beethoven regretted publishing because he was dissatisfied with Jesus' harsh treatment after he left the Mount of Olives. It was too emotionally raw of a piece for him to share with the world, and he wished in retrospect that he hadn't. Nevertheless, it would stir the heart of the future American leader.

When Condi first enrolled at the University of Denver, she planned to only attend for a year and then transfer, but her mother's fight with cancer and her desire to be close to both her parents kept her there until she graduated.

During Condi's junior year, at the tender age of eighteen she was approached to be a student mentor in the College Acquaintance Recruitment Experience (CARE) at the university, and she jumped at the chance. While not yet a graduate of the university, but already accepted into the graduate program of international relations at Notre Dame, Condi's role was to provide necessary counseling services for prospective students, specifically minority students, who wanted to know about the University of Denver. Although her schedule was often more than full, Condi always found time to talk with prospective students on the phone, arrange a tour of the campus, and meet with them as needed.

In November 1971 John confronted apparent racism in regard to the lack of minority staff at the University of Denver head-on in the college paper, the *Clarion*, stating, "At DU we ought to be alert, searching continually for minority faculty. There ought to be a 12 month program; there ought to be people who are geared to seek out and find blacks and browns. Right now colleges across the nation are graduating more blacks and browns than ever before. How many of these schools have we contacted? Have we sent anyone there? Is anybody looking for them? It's sad, but I think not. It seems as if we cannot find blacks. These people are out there; they are ready; they can be hired. They are in many instances superior to many of the people we presently have on campus and we ought to go out and find them. If we at DU are going to allow racism to be part of our institution, one of the things we are going to have to do is take the blame for allowing the destruction of our country."

The University of Denver took John's words to heart and began to advocate for the hiring of more minorities. As a result of his determination and perseverance on the issue, John was awarded a bust of a large, black fist, representing the strength and support he displayed in his association with the University of Denver. He also received an honorary membership to the Muwi Wazuri (Swahili for "beautiful black man"), and shortly after this honor he was given the job as associate dean of arts and sciences at Denver University.

During an Aspen summer camp for pianists in her sophomore year of college, Condi realized that some children there were much younger than her but more talented. She met eleven-year-olds who could play from sight what had taken her twelve months to learn. She recalled that Mozart didn't have to practice and that despite the fact that she had been practicing day in and day out, she would never be more than "just pretty good," and pretty good wouldn't lead her to a career on the concert stage. As a matter of fact, she feared she would end up merely being an accompanist, playing in a piano bar, or teaching children to murder Beethoven for a living.

"I woke up one day—literally—and thought, 'This is not for me.' I was talented but not exceptionally talented, and I lacked that . . . discipline that you need to be a really fine musician."[8]

She has also stated, "I thought of listening to all those never-ending scales and trying to teach sulky children who refused to practice at home. I looked around for some other career."[9]

Condi wrestled with what to do. Her talent and dream of becoming a concert pianist had brought discussion between her and her parents about attending Juilliard. By all external evidence, she was supposed to be a music major—after all, she was able to read music before she could read books—but she also recognized that she didn't have the necessary talent or passion for practicing to hone her art. She felt she had to change her major—and fast. But first she'd have to tell her parents.

John and Angelena had spent a fortune helping Condi fulfill what they thought was her dream—to be a concert pianist—and had bought her that $13,000 Steinway, and she was worried about how they'd react to the news. Still, she went to them boldly, telling them she was changing her major. They were shocked and resistant.

John and Angelena encouraged Condi to continue studying

music until she found something she'd rather study. In evaluating her interests, Condi knew she had a passion for politics because of her upbringing in Birmingham. Additionally, she felt strongly that her race needed to become part of the larger world, to become involved in issues confronting all Americans. It didn't take long for her to discover her new calling. One day she wandered into a course in international politics taught by Josef Korbel. He had served as an advisor to Edvard Benes, the exiled Czech president who lived in London until the Nazis were defeated. After World War II the Korbel family moved to Belgrade, Czechoslovakia where Korbel served as the country's ambassador to Yugoslavia.

In 1948 the Korbel family was forced to flee again when the Communists assumed power over Czechoslovakia. After learning that he had been tried and sentenced to death *in absentia*, Korbel was granted political asylum in the United States. He was hired to teach international politics at the University of Denver and became the dean of international studies.

Condi relates, "I learned that I had an inexplicable love for things Russian, that an adopted culture can teach you a great deal about yourself."

When Condi went to her parents and shared her newfound love, she was met with surprise and further resistance. John tried desperately to reason with his daughter, telling her that black people don't make money in political science. But Condi was prepared. "Music either, Daddy," she answered. "Music either."

The Development of a
Soviet Expert

$\mathcal{C}$ ondi's passion for Russia seemed to have come out of nowhere, and for the next eighteen months Russia's history permeated her every waking moment. She quickly learned the language and began inundating herself with Russian media, even reading *Pravda*, the Soviet newspaper, on a daily basis. Shortly thereafter she began studying the Moscow press and military journals. She even named her car Boris after the country's leader, Boris Yeltsin.

While mentoring Condi about Russia, Josef Korbel was also successfully mentoring another influential woman—his daughter Madeleine.

Madeleine had been born Marie Jana Korbelova in Prague, Czechoslovakia (now the Czech Republic) on May 15, 1937 and was raised Roman Catholic by her parents, who had converted to Catholicism from Judaism in order to escape persecution.

Madeleine attended school in Switzerland and then in Denver where her father taught. Later she majored in political science after receiving a scholarship at Wellesley College in Massachusetts, graduating in 1959, two years after she became a United States citizen. While working for the *Denver Post* one summer, Madeleine met and married Chicago newspaper journalist Joseph Medill Patterson Albright.

Madeleine was extremely intelligent and learned easily. She gave birth to a daughter, then got pregnant with twins who were born six weeks prematurely. While the babies were in incubators trying to survive, she took a course in Russian as a distraction. By the end of their hospital stay, she was fluent in the language. While raising her family, she earned a Ph.D. in public law and government from Columbia University.

Condi and Madeleine had a lot in common besides having Korbel for a mentor. Both their relatives fought hard for democracy. They were both raised facing severe prejudice, have a passion for the Slav people, are multilingual, are very intelligent, and have an extensive interest in Russia and the Russian language. Additionally they were both very close to their fathers. As a result of Madeleine's bond with her father, she followed closely in his footsteps in regard to her career. Ironically, although both women were mentored by the same man, they each took different courses in life and would stand on opposite sides politically, although they would share the title of Secretary of State.

As he had done with his daughter Madeleine, Josef Korbel took the young college student Condi under his wing and provided extensive mentoring and knowledge about Russia and the Slav people to feed the fire that had been kindled within her heart. Her newfound interest in Russia consumed her day and night. It stirred a passion within her that led to compassion for its people. Condi described the transition from being a music major to Soviet studies as falling in love and as an experience she'd never had before. And just like any new love, Condi's whole life revolved around the Soviet Union. She'd study that people's history for hours outside of her class requirements, learning everything she could about the historically Communist-ridden nation.

When Condi became old enough to register to vote, she became a Republican, she says, for different reasons than her father who had joined the party over twenty years earlier.

"Our Party's principles made me a Republican," she said. "The first Republican I knew was my father. He joined our party because the Democrats in Jim Crow Alabama of 1952 would not register him to vote. The Republicans did. I joined for different reasons. I found a party that sees me as an individual, not as part of a group. I found a party that puts family first. I found a party that has love of liberty at its core. And I found a party that believes that peace begins with strength."[1]

In 1972, Condi's senior year of college, the Equal Employment Opportunity Act was passed to ensure fair treatment to all segments of society without regard to race, religion, color, national origin, or sex. The goal of this law and program was to make discrimination in employment illegal and would eventually include affirmative action programs as well as the process of and remedies for discrimination complaints.

As a result of inundating herself with all things Russian, Condi ceased taking as good of care of her appearance as she once did. A self-proclaimed lover of fried foods and salt, her undisciplined eating habits in conjunction with a lack of exercise put an extra thirty pounds on the small-boned twenty-year-old. The 5'7" athlete hated how that made her feel and the lack of energy that accompanied the extra weight. So she promptly began an exercise program and healthier eating habits that would help her lose the excess pounds.

Somewhere along this time frame, Condi met and began dating Rick Upchurch, two years her senior. Condi and Rick were the epitome of "opposites attract." She had been raised by her parents in a safe and secure home, while Rick had been raised by his grandparents. Condi was spoon-fed Beethoven and Mozart growing up, and he broke his teeth surviving in the impoverished streets of Holland, Ohio, a suburb of Toledo. She was given every opportunity to succeed in life, and all the odds of success were stacked against Rick from the beginning. They did have, however, two very important things in common: perseverance and football.

Rick had been very close to his grandparents while growing up since he lived with them. So when his grandmother died when he was in the sixth grade, his already fragile world began to fall apart around him. His grandfather continued to raise him but passed away due to cancer when Rick was a junior at Springfield High School, leaving the fledgling teen to care for himself.

Rick had always been an athlete and along with football played baseball, basketball, and track. While he was successful in each sport, his passion and vision for success was found on the high-school football field where he was a champion in the making. Rick was All-League, All-District, and Co-player of the year repeatedly, and in his senior year he was instrumental in leading his team to their first state championship ever.

After his grandfather's death, two families stepped in to help Rick finish high school. He received a sports scholarship from Indian Hills Junior College in Centerville, Iowa. While at Indian Hills, Rick was the first player in their history to be a two-time Junior College All-American.

From Indian Hills, Rick earned his Bachelor of Arts from the University of Minnesota, where he continued to break records and would eventually be inducted into that college's Football Hall of Fame. While at the University of Minnesota Rich was signed by a scout for the Denver Broncos.

Although Condi and Rick would eventually become engaged, then permanently break up, both would go on to become highly successful in life.

In his rookie season with the Broncos, Rick rushed for ninety-seven yards, caught eighteen passes for 436 yards, returned twenty-seven punts for 312 yards, and added another 1,014 yards returning kickoffs. In his second season he set an NFL record by returning four punts for touchdowns and made it to the Pro Bowl (as he did three other times). He also played in a Super Bowl during his career.

In the meantime, in 1973 John Rice became the assistant vice chancellor for the University Resources Department, and Angelena continued to work in the administration office at the University of Denver and to get treatment for the cancer her body was fighting. The following summer, Condi graduated number one in her class— Phi Beta Kappa (cum laude with honors)—from the University of Denver at the age of nineteen with a Bachelor's degree in political science and absolutely no idea what she was going to do with it. She did know, however, that the job market had to be brighter for political scientists than it was for concert pianists.

Although her parents had been resistant about her changing her major from music to political science, she knew they were proud of her accomplishment.

"I will always remember my undergraduate commencement at the University of Denver. I remember the pride of my family. I remember the closeness I felt to my classmates and friends. I remember the thrill that comes with reaching any important goal. I do not, however, remember a single word that my commencement speaker said."[2]

After attaining her Bachelor's degree, Condi knew that she was not the same person she had been four years earlier when she was taking classes in high school. The experience of going to college and the education she'd attained had transformed her. It imparted knowledge and expanded her horizons, making her a better, wiser, more compassionate person. It broke the barriers of race and class and allowed her to make herself anew. And just as she'd learned from the stories her father told her about her Granddaddy Rice, Condi knew that education was a privilege, and with privilege comes responsibility. Like all of her family who have worked hard to obtain an education, she has strong feelings about her accomplishment and the responsibility that she and others with college degrees have to the world. In understanding her perspective regarding the responsibility of the educated individual, we learn a lot about her values and the way she deals with people and situations she comes across every day.

"The first responsibility of the educated person is to be optimistic. Cynicism and pessimism are too often the companions of learning. There have indeed been dark chapters in the human story—and the more we learn about history's failures and cruelties, the more our minds can be tempted to despair. But for all of our problems today, and by just about every measure, the world is a better, more hopeful place than it ever has been.

"The advances that have been made during [my lifetime] alone—from breakthroughs in health care, to the spread of prosperity, to the progress of democracy—have been pushed along by optimists, not pessimists. America's founders were not pessimists. Nor were the Wright Brothers, or Jonas Salk, or Martin Luther King. Nor is any man or woman of real accomplishment. The reason is simple—pessimism is the easy way out. It is characteristic of those content to stand on the sidelines and watch the march of history. Optimism requires work.

"It requires examination and objective thought. Optimists move and shape history because those with a vision of a better world have the energy and discipline required to make those visions real . . . progress is not only possible, but an unfolding story in which [the educated] have an obligation to play a part.

"Second, you also have an obligation to remember those who weren't as lucky as you. It is natural—especially among the educated—to credit one's good fortune to one's intelligence, hard work, and judgment. And, in fact, it is certainly true that [the educated] possess these qualities. But it is also true that merit alone did not see you to [attaining a degree].

"There are many people in this country . . . who are just as intelligent, just as hard-working, and just as deserving. But, for whatever reason, they did not enjoy all of the opportunities that came [my] way. . . . Just because you deserve something does not necessarily mean that you will get it.

"Third, the educated have an obligation to work to close the cultural gaps that divide our nation and our world. In the wake of [terrorist] attacks, it would have been easy, in our grief and our anger, to retreat behind a wall of defeatism and discrimination. But that is not the American way. We did not close our borders to the tens of thousands of students from Muslim countries seeking to study here. Even as we have done the necessary and important work of improving our visa screening, we have continued to welcome people from other nations and we need to do more to let people know that they are indeed welcome. This response says a lot about our nation. At a fundamental level, it underscores our faith in diversity and individual rights.

"The intellectual foundation of terrorism—just like that of slavery and segregation—rests on arbitrarily dividing the human race into friends and enemies, even human and non-human. . . . Perpetrators of [terrorist attacks] were people who believed that differences are a license to kill.

"Fourth, the educated have an obligation not to let your education and good luck lead you into false pride or condescension. All people are bound together by several common desires. Never make the mistake of assuming that some people do not share your desire to live freely . . . to think and believe as they see fit . . . to raise a family and educate their children. Never make the mistake of assuming that some people do not desire the freedom to chart their own courses in life.

"I have listened with disbelief as some explained why Russians would never embrace freedom . . . that military dictatorship would always be a way of life in Latin America . . . that Asian values were incompatible with democracy . . . and that tyranny, corruption, and one-party rule would always dominate the African continent.

"Finally, let me close with the obligations you have to yourself. I encourage [the educated] to do two things: First, do not rest until you find your passion. I don't mean merely something that interests you—but your calling; your life's work. Not something you have to do each day, but that thing which you can't do without each day. Something that you love enough and care about enough that it makes you glad to be alive.

"... Throughout the world it is a privilege to have an education. It is a club that you may never quit, and from which you can never be expelled. And membership confers responsibilities that you must fulfill. You have the responsibility to better your world—a task that requires optimism. You have a responsibility to those less fortunate than you—to mentor them and support their efforts to better themselves. You have a responsibility to close the divides between cultures.

"In these ways, you will satisfy the obligations of education. And in the process, you will bring your privilege to bear on the challenges of our world. H. G. Wells said that history is a race between education and catastrophe."[3]

Condi's words have a depth to them that rings true and are a compilation of core beliefs that originated with her grandfathers, were passed down through her parents, and even now reveal the heart of her integrity.

From the University of Denver, Condi became a first-year Graduate Fellow at the University of Notre Dame and earned her Master's degree in political science in just fourteen months. Fellow students and friends could already see that she was on her way to being a Soviet specialist as she consumed herself with everything she could find on the topic and was often engaging in conversations with her professors after class regarding Russia.

Because of her scholastic success, Condi applied and was accepted by several law schools and went back to Denver with the intention of entering law school there. But she was never sold on the idea. At what seemed like the last minute, she decided to take a year off from attending law school while she found the right direction for her career and ended up taking a number of courses at the Independent School for International Studies at the University of Denver. Additionally she was a fellow at the Denver Social Science

Foundation, and in 1977 Condi was offered a National Fund Fellowship for Outstanding Minority Graduate Students.

As she completed classes at the Independent School for International Studies, she decided to further her education. "I realized that I liked political science more than law, and I sort of stumbled into a Ph.D. program."[4]

As Korbel continued to educate and mentor both his daughter Madeleine and Condi, the two foreign policy prodigies took different political routes. Madeleine would go on to be a lifelong Democrat who would serve under President William Clinton, and Condi is a Republican who would eventually serve in different roles in the administration of two Republican Presidents. Both women, however, would blaze a wide trail for women in the predominantly male foreign policy arena.

In 1977, when Condi was twenty-three and began to work on her Ph.D. at the University of Denver, Josef Korbel unexpectedly died. Although his legacy would go on through his daughter Madeleine and eventually through Condi, he was sorely missed by those whom he had taught and mentored. Nonetheless, both Madeleine and Condi would go on to make him proud of the work and passion he instilled in both of them.

The following year the United States Postal Service issued the Black Heritage Postage Stamp Series commemorating and giving tribute to African-Americans who strived to liberate themselves from the chains of slavery and segregation.

By 1980 Condi had successfully earned a Ph.D. from the Graduate School of International Studies (Soviet politics and culture). Her love for music did not wane during her political studies, as she continued to regularly attend music camps and play at various recitals. She even found ways to mix both her loves. Her yearlong independent project for international studies was on "Music and Politics in the Soviet Union."

During this season of her life Condi traveled to Eastern Europe where she stayed for seven weeks. She visited the Soviet Union and was briefly in Poland getting hands-on knowledge and experience with the people she'd come to adore. During this same season of her life, Condi was a Ford Foundation Fellow and a Stanford University Arms Control Fellow.

"I was interested in the state power of the Soviet Union rather than ideology, and that was continued right along. Also, in graduate school I had met a number of émigré Slavs. My mentor was Josef Korbel. . . . My Russian teacher was also a Czech. With all these influences and my reading, I developed a strong feeling for the Slavic people.

"Ironically, [my love for the Slavic people] may have started in 1968, a year that was a crack in time. That was the year Bobby Kennedy and Martin Luther King were shot. But the event that really struck me was the Soviet invasion of Czechoslovakia. I can still feel the strong sense I had of remorse and regret that a brave people had been subdued.

"I remember wondering what sort of man was Dubcek, the Czech president. I recall seeing pictures of Soviet tanks rolling into Prague and being appalled by this exercise of naked power.

"Earlier my interest in military policy may have been heightened by the Cuban missile crisis, which I remember vividly, though I was barely eight years old. Those Soviet missiles were within range of the southeastern U.S., and for a young child, news reports to that effect were frightening."[5] She adds, "We all lived within range. The Southeast was it—you'd see these red arrows coming at Birmingham. And I remember thinking that was something that maybe my father couldn't handle."[6]

The Cuban Missile Crisis had occurred in October 1962 when, after reviewing newly acquired intelligence, President John F. Kennedy informed the world that the Soviet Union was building secret missile bases in Cuba, a mere ninety miles off the shores of Florida. It was a direct threat to America and her people.

After weighing various options such as invading Cuba and sending in planes to do air strikes against the missiles, the President decided to simply demand that Russian premier Nikita S. Khrushchev remove all the missile bases and their deadly contents. He hoped a nonaggressive and nonviolent approach would avoid putting Khrushchev on the defense. The President further ordered a naval quarantine or blockade of Cuba in order to prevent Russian ships from bringing additional missiles and construction materials to the island.

In response to the American naval blockade, Khrushchev authorized his Soviet field commanders in Cuba to launch their tactical nuclear weapons if invaded by United States forces. Deadlocked in this manner, the two leaders of the world's greatest nuclear superpowers had a showdown and played chicken for seven days. Finally on October 28 Khrushchev's heart softened, and he conceded to President Kennedy's demands by ordering all Soviet supply ships away from Cuban waters and agreed to remove the missiles from Cuba's mainland. The crisis could have resulted in a nuclear holocaust, but by the grace of God Khrushchev backed down, an answer to the prayer of many believers.

The Cuban Missile Crisis scared Condi. Even at eight years old she knew enough to realize that she and her family lived in range of the missiles. In the midst of the most heated racism Birmingham experienced, she had not been scared, believing that her parents could and would protect her. But when the Cuban Missile Crisis occurred, she knew it was more than her father could handle with a simple explanation. As many families did on that occasion, the Rices prayed for a peaceful resolution.

Condi received several fellowships from many prestigious schools after earning her Ph.D. She'd made a successful transformation from pianist to Soviet expert and was fluent in both. Condi considered the many options open to her and accepted a one-year fellowship at Stanford University's Center for International Security and Arms Control. The center had never admitted female fellows before, let alone a black female fellow. Furthermore, it had never accepted anyone from the University of Denver (as opposed to a more elite graduate program). But Stanford had received some heat for having a lack of faculty that was both female and minority; so they were willing to step outside their usual requirements. Additionally, Condi's fellowship would be paid for with university funds reserved for minority faculty.

Condi was honored by the invitation for the fellowship and moved from Denver to Palo Alto, California. At twenty-six she was an assistant professor at one of the most progressive and prestigious universities in the world, teaching classes in Soviet and East European foreign and defense policy, comparative study of military institutions, and international security policy. She was definitely in her element.

During Condi's transition to California, Sandra Day O'Connor became the first woman to be appointed to the United States Supreme Court, and a visible shift occurred in the government, preparing a way for God's plans for Condi to be fulfilled.

Although God was evident in Condi's life, it was a time of spiritual struggle for her. "Although I never doubted the existence of God, I think like all people I've had some ups and downs in my faith. When I first moved to California in 1981 to join the faculty at Stanford, there were a lot of years when I was not attending church regularly. I was a specialist in international politics, so I was always traveling abroad. I was always in another time zone."

Condi says that she was too busy to go to church, and slowly but surely the faith that had always been so precious to her faded into the background. Knowing that God had not left her, she also knew that he was not front and center in the way she'd lived her life before and after going to Stanford.

"One Sunday I was in the Lucky's Supermarket not very far from my house—I will never forget—among the spices—an African-American man walked up to me and said he was buying some things for his church picnic. And he said, 'Do you play the piano by any chance?'

"I said, 'Yes.' He said they were looking for someone to play the piano at church. It was a little African-American church right in the center of Palo Alto. A Baptist church. So I started playing for that church. That got me regularly back into churchgoing."

The man Condi ran into that Sunday morning was Dale Hamel, a longtime member of Jerusalem Baptist Church and then president of the choir. According to him, they practically bumped into one another. He noticed her long fingers and the absence of a ring on her wedding ring finger and immediately inquired about her abilities as a pianist. He laughs when asked if he was looking for a pianist or a date but says that he had no idea God was using him as an instrument in the life of another soul who had become too busy for God. It would prove to be a time of stretching for Condi—for her career, faith, and musical talents.

Lori White, a close friend of Condi, laughs as she tells how Condi struggled to play for the Baptist church.

"Condi doesn't play gospel, she's a concert pianist. Black ministers in Baptist churches don't follow the music—they follow the spirit, and Condi was having a hard time keeping up."

Condi knew how to read music but was not familiar with the unconventional ways of worship in the rich and often unorthodox Baptist denomination. She knew, however, that her mother could help her. Angelena had played the piano for Baptist churches before; so Condi called her mother and asked for her advice. As she laughed, Angelena advised her daughter to play in the chord of C, and then the choir would follow her lead—and she was right. The next time Condi got into a spiritual jam playing for the Baptist church, she played in the chord of C, and the hymn-singing choir followed her every step.

For a young girl who never questioned the existence of God, she was still surprised by God's intervention in her life to get her back on track spiritually. "I thought to myself, 'My goodness, God has a long reach,'" she says. "I mean, in the Lucky's Supermarket on a Sunday morning amongst the spices. As a result of going there and playing and getting involved again with the church community, I began to see how much of my faith . . . I'd taken for granted."[7]

Condi sensed God speaking directly to her through that situation, challenging her to take her faith in him more seriously, which she did.

Condi was appreciative of Dale Hamel's obedience to stop and talk to her that Sunday morning in the Lucky's Supermarket spice aisle, but she was a devoted Presbyterian, missed the governance structure of that church, and wanted to get back to her roots. After playing piano for Jerusalem Baptist Church for about six months she found and began to attend Menlo Park Presbyterian Church in Palo Alto, not far from the city of Stanford where the university was located. It was the church home of many of the faculty and high-profile, faith-based leaders in California. There at Menlo Park Presbyterian God continued to speak to her and encourage her in her spiritual walk.

"On a Sunday morning, the minister gave a sermon I will never quite forget. It was about the Prodigal Son from the point of view of the elder son. It set the elder son up not as somebody who had done all the right things but as somebody who had become so self-satisfied—a parable about self-satisfaction and contentment and complacency in faith—that people who didn't somehow expect themselves to need to be born again can be so complacent.

"I started to think of myself as that elder son who had never doubted the existence of the Heavenly Father but wasn't really walking in faith in an active way anymore. I started to become more active with the church, to go to Bible study and to have a more active prayer life. It was a very important turning point in my life."[8]

It was a necessary turning point in her life. What Condoleezza didn't know was that the following years would be some of the hardest she'd ever experienced and that God was preparing her to be able to deal with them. He needed her to shift her dependence from her intelligence and ability to handle life on her terms onto him.

8

THE STANFORD YEARS

The 1980s were a busy season for the Rices and brought them a lot of change. John Rice retired from the University of Denver in 1982, and two years later Condoleezza became widely known as an expert in Soviet politics and began to travel frequently. Additionally she served on the Board of Directors for Mid-Peninsula Urban Coalition and the MacArthur Fellowship in International Security Selection Committee and was on the Presidential Committee for the selection of the vice president and provost at Stanford.

Condi continued to lecture students on political science and won Stanford University's highest honor for teaching, the Walter J. Gores Award for Excellence in Teaching. She has perhaps never been as proud of any accomplishment as this honor because it was awarded to her by her students who had voted on her behalf.

Students spoke of her contagious enthusiasm, her exhaustive knowledge of a subject, her thorough preparation, the clarity of her lectures, and her ability to inspire lively discussion in seminars. Her course evaluations showed her to be above the university mean on all counts and reflected the enthusiasm expressed in her teaching. Just knowing that her students and parents watched as she accepted that coveted award meant the world to her. "It was one of the greatest thrills of my life," she says. "I could see many of my students cheering for me."[1]

In 1983 Martin Luther King, Jr. Day was first celebrated by the United States as a federal holiday, and Colonel Guion "Guy" Bluford became the first African-American astronaut. America was continuing to stretch and grow.

The next year Condi published her first book, *Uncertain Allegiance: The Soviet Union and the Czechoslovak Army*, with Princeton University Press. Condi was on a career high. Her hard work at completing school was worth it as her career boomed above any and all expectations. God's favor on her was apparent and would continue.

In 1984 Stanford sponsored the Bellagio "New Faces" Conference, sponsored by the Arms Control Association and The International Institute for Strategic Studies, and Condi was asked to be a delegate and to speak on the Soviet Union. It was there that she met Brent Scowcroft, who had been invited by the university to talk about arms control. Scowcroft had been the United States National Security Advisor under President Gerald Ford and both general and lieutenant general in the United States Air Force. He also served as military assistant to President Richard Nixon and as deputy assistant to the President for National Security Affairs in the Nixon and Ford Administrations. He was also the vice chairman of Kissinger and Associates, the founder and president of The Forum for International Policy, a think tank, and a member of the Council on Foreign Relations.

At that time Condi was almost thirty years old and already an expert on the Eastern bloc military. In his talk Scowcroft said something that Condi disagreed with, and she challenged his work. Scowcroft was immediately taken with Condi's boldness and knowledge on the topic, engaged in further conversation with her, and was impressed. He resolved to help Condi advance in her career, and almost immediately she became his informal protégé.

Scowcroft was a member of the elite Aspen Institute, an organization made up of a group of twenty leaders whose mission is to foster enlightened leadership and open-minded dialogue through seminars, policy programs, conferences, and leadership development initiatives. Scowcroft was so impressed with Condi that he invited her to join a foreign policy group at the Aspen Institute, and she was soon extended a much coveted membership.

While her career was taking off, Condi's personal life was struggling. The Rice family found out that Angelena's cancer had returned—with a vengeance—and unfortunately had made it to various lymph nodes.

Naturally the family was devastated. John was immobilized in many ways, and Angelena's prospective death threw him into severe anticipatory grief. God had graciously given John and Condi fifteen more years with Angelena than they'd expected after she'd been diagnosed with breast cancer in 1970. But this time they all knew that Angelena's health was growing worse and that she would not recover.

Condi's greatest fear was becoming a reality. She was losing her best friend and source of inspiration. It was something that was inevitable, but something Condi knew would be the hardest thing she'd ever have to go through. In June 1985 Angelena Rice lost her battle with breast cancer, and the rubber hit the road in the spiritual life of Condoleezza.

Condi was in California when she got the news of her mother's death. She immediately bought a plane ticket to return to Denver for the memorial service but wasn't leaving Palo Alto until the following day.

"What was I going to do without my mother?" she wondered. "What would replace our nightly telephone calls? She was only sixty-one years old, and no intellect could soothe the hurt that was there."[2]

Condi was so devastated by her mother's death that she called a good friend and colleague from Stanford, Coit "Chip" Blacker, at 12:30 in the morning and asked him to come to her home and talk with her, which he did immediately. As one would expect with the loss of a parent and being thousands of miles away from family, Condi needed someone with whom to talk. Coit comforted his friend as she cried on his shoulder, and he stayed with Condi through the night for support. At 7 in the morning when she was ready to go to the airport, Coit noticed that she was unusually calm and asked her how she could be after such a loss. She looked him in the eyes and told him it was because she was sure that she'd see her mother again someday in heaven.

Condi was forced to cling to her faith so the grief wouldn't consume her. She was highly intelligent, but being bright couldn't help her grapple with her anguish. She had to find another way to cope.

"I knew that I would not be able to move beyond her death because of my intellect, and certainly not by the power of reason," Condoleezza shares honestly. "Instead, I would have to trust God's Word, press in closer to him, and rest in the peace that surpasses all understanding. Only my faith in God could bridge the gap between what I was feeling and what I needed to do in dealing with my grief. I was blessed to have had seeds of faith planted in my soul about God's faithfulness from my childhood to fall back on."[3]

For Condi, the loss of her mother meant the loss of the person whose advice she valued most in the world, her source of encouragement, her refuge, her best friend, her confidant. It was her mother's love for the Lord and for music that had planted seeds in Condi's life and had first given her a passion for music and the goal of becoming a concert pianist, and now she was gone. But despite the pain Condi also saw the hidden blessing amidst the agony.

"I was blessed that she was able to see me finish college and teach at Stanford. I won the Walter J. Gores Award for Excellence in Teaching, and both my parents were able to attend and see me receive it in person. What a blessing those fifteen [extra] years were."

Condi returned to Palo Alto after her mother's funeral, leaving her father behind in Denver. As is the case when a person grieves, there were times in the days, weeks, and months that followed when the burden became too heavy for Condi to carry on her own. As a result she was forced again and again to cling to God and recalls being filled with his strength—the strength that the Bible promises will surpass all understanding in her darkest hours.

"The peace and love of God is real," Condi shares openly. She focused on the Bible and on God's promises in the aftermath of the loss of her mother. She also knew that in order to be a recipient of that peace, she had to open her heart and let God in as opposed to closing it in anger toward him for taking her mother and receiving no comfort from him.

Looking back, she can see how God used that time to fortify his relationship with her and bring an intimacy to their relationship that is too often missing in many of the lives of individuals who tend to overintellectualize life. Looking back on those days of bereavement, Condi says, she can now see that her time of grieving was a privilege for her in many ways, and she encourages others to be optimistic in the midst of suffering.

"It is in times like these that we are reminded of a paradox, that it is a privilege to struggle. American slaves used to sing, 'Nobody knows the trouble I've seen—Glory Hallelujah!' Growing up, I would often wonder at the seeming contradiction contained in this line. But as I grew older, I came to learn that there is no contradiction at all.

"I believe this same message is found in the Bible in Romans 5, where we are told to 'rejoice in our sufferings, knowing that suffering produces endurance, and endurance produces character, and character produces hope, and hope does not disappoint us, because God's love has been poured into our hearts through the Holy Spirit which has been given to us.'

"For me, this message has two lessons. First, there is the lesson that only through struggle do we realize the depths of our resilience and understand that the hardest of blows can be survived and overcome. Too often when all is well, we slip into the false joy and satisfaction of the material and a complacent pride and faith in ourselves. Yet it is through struggle that we find redemption and self-knowledge. In this sense it is a privilege to struggle because it frees one from the idea that the human spirit is fragile, like a house of cards, or that human strength is fleeting. It is this belief in the resilience of the human spirit that I believe the Apostle Paul affirmed more beautifully than any before him or any since. Locked in a prison, Paul warned off those who would feel sorry for him. To the Philippians, Paul wrote: 'I have learned in whatever state I am, to be content: I know how to be abased and I know how to abound. Everywhere and in all things I have learned both to be full and to be hungry, both to abound and to suffer need' (Phil. 4:11-12). As Paul taught in this brilliant passage, finding peace in the midst of pain is the true fulfillment of one's humility, and the relationship with God is complete.

"[I] first learned this truth [after] the death of my mother. My mother had cancer for many years. As a matter of fact, she first had cancer when I was 15 years old. My father and I prayed that she might live to see me grow up and, indeed, she lived until I was 30—quite a very big difference between 15 and 30. That prayer was answered. But as you might imagine, as I got older, knowing that this threat of cancer was hanging over us, I feared her death in the abstract almost every day. I could not fathom in the abstract how I could survive her death. But when she died—though I miss her to this very day more than I could have ever imagined—I did, nonetheless, find the strength to go on. And I understood for the very first time in my life something I had heard in church many, many times: 'The peace that surpasses all understanding.' It is in those times when the intellect, when human will, when the ability to understand with our feeble minds cannot serve us that the spirit takes over and somehow we survive.

"We see this theme illustrated in sacred texts the world over. In the Book of Job, God tests Job's faith by taking from him everything that he cherishes—his wealth, his health, and his family. Early in his trials, one of Job's friends counsels him to be patient, saying, 'Behold, happy is the man whom God correcteth; therefore despise not thou the chastening of the Almighty: For he maketh sore, and bindeth up: he woundeth, and his hands make whole. . . . In famine he shall redeem thee from death; and in war from the power of the sword. . . . And thou shalt know that thy tabernacle shall be in peace. . . .' In the end, Job's sufferings strengthen his faith and, we are told, he is rewarded with 'twice as much as he had before' and he lived 'a hundred and forty years' until he was 'old and full of days.' We learn in times of personal struggle—the loss of a loved one, illness, or turmoil—that there is a peace that passeth understanding. When our intellect is unequal to the task, the spirit takes over; finding peace in the midst of pain is the true fulfillment of one's humanity.

"Struggle doesn't just strengthen us to survive hard times—it is also the key foundation for true optimism and accomplishment. Indeed, personal achievement without struggle somehow feels incomplete and hollow. It is true too for humankind—because nothing of lasting value has ever been achieved without sacrifice.

"There is a second, more important, lesson to be learned from struggle and suffering . . . that we can use the strength it gives us for the good of others. Nothing good is born of personal struggle if it is used to fuel one's sense of entitlement, or superiority to those who we perceive to have struggled less than we. Everyone has been blessed, and I am sure we all know that it is dangerous to think about the hand that one has been dealt relative to others if it ends in questioning why someone else has more. It is, on the other hand, sobering and humbling to think about one's blessings and to ask why you have been given so much when others have so little.

"Our goal must not be to get through a struggle so that others can congratulate us on our resilience, nor is it to dwell on struggle as a badge of honor. Perhaps this is why in describing his personal struggle, the Apostle Paul felt it necessary to say to the Philippians,

'Forgetting those things that are behind and reaching forward to those things which are ahead . . . I press toward the goal for the prize of the upward call of God in Christ Jesus.'

"But to direct the energies from our struggle toward the good of others, we must first let go of the pain, and the bad memories, and the sense of unfairness—of 'Why me?'—that inevitably accompany deep personal turmoil."[4]

Angelena's sickness and death was a sudden surprise for many. The Rices hadn't shared her first bout with cancer with many people. It was a family issue and predominantly remained a family issue for the sake of privacy.

As John mourned, he too went through the normal stages of grief and became confused and angry toward God for taking Angelena.

"John called me and told me Angelena had passed," remembers Moses Brewer, "and I was shocked. John didn't tell us when Angelena got sick the first time. He kept that stuff a secret because it was a family issue. When we talked that day, he said, 'Do you know, Mo, life is a chore. Condi's in good shape now, and has finished her Ph.D. from the University and now we don't have to worry about finances anymore, and we were just looking so forward to this day and now she's gone.'

"I was worried about him," remembers Brewer. "I just knew it was all over for him when she passed away. I knew he wouldn't survive."

But John did survive. Like his daughter, he clung to his faith, knowing that if he even loosened his grip he might be consumed with grief and it would be the end.

"For a year or two after her mother's death John was really just a shell of his former self," shares Lori White, friend of the Rice family. "Condi suggested to him that he move to California, but she really wasn't quite sure how all that was going to play out. She had to work and was worried about caring for him, but she also knew her father needed her."

"From what he told me," remembers family friend Annye Marie Downing, "John didn't want to go to California to live, but he wanted to be with his daughter, and she wanted him to be with her."

Eventually John did move to California to be near Condi and immediately threw himself into what he was best at—mentoring youth. John became involved with various programs for youth, looking for ways to mentor and encourage minorities.

"Condi was really amazed that her dad got to California, got his own apartment, started developing his own personal network, and eventually became himself again," remembers White. "She really admired her dad. He was an older man when this happened, but he was really able to re-create a life for himself."

John made a natural, healthy transition through his grief by his own dependence on God and by being around Condi, but friends say he never fully got back to being the John they knew before Angelena's death. Despite the age difference, father and daughter were learning the same valuable spiritual lesson: God is just as faithful in the valleys as he is on the mountaintops.

THE SCOWCROFT YEARS

*W*ithin a year after her mother's death, Condoleezza published her second book, *The Gorbachev Era* (Stanford Alumni Press), with Alexander Dallin, and accepted the position of Consultant to the Joint Chiefs of Staff at the Pentagon, where she would work on nuclear strategic planning as part of a Council on Foreign Relations fellowship. Additionally, she was on the Council on Foreign Relations and was an International Affairs Fellow at Hoover.

After her fellowships were completed in 1988, Condi moved back to Palo Alto, California to become an associate professor of political science at Stanford University. She threw herself into the things she loved the most—teaching, athletics, entertaining friends, and music—and served again on the Board of Directors for the Mid-Peninsula Urban Coalition.

Brent Scowcroft, who had become close to his protégé, joked that Condi returned to California to find a husband and raise a family. "I really failed if that was my plan," Condi replied to Scowcroft's assumptions.[1]

When Condi wasn't at Stanford educating a room full of college students, she was working out with the varsity football team at Stanford or with their coach who also spent one-on-one time training her. She also played the piano twice a month with an informal chamber music group, attended various music performances, and had informal dinners and get-togethers with friends.

As John settled into California and got his bearings, he went to various school sites to see what programs existed in the community and where he could pick up the slack for minority boys and girls whose needs were not being met. During one of these visits John met the executive director of the Boys and Girls Club, Jackie Glaster, and they began talking about different ideas he had for underprivileged children.

Glaster was impressed with John's success in Denver and Alabama and immediately liked the person she fondly calls "the big, burly black man." John and Glaster quickly became friends.

"John was an incredible man," she remembers. "He was very religious, a very strong believer in God, and spiritual. We would have a lot of wonderful discussions over breakfast. He would talk about how he'd have these conversations with God about all the ideas that were going on in his head. He had wonderful communication with God, and I admired him."

Once or twice a month John and Glaster would meet over breakfast and discuss the many programs available for minority children in the area, and John quickly became a mentor and confidant to her. Everywhere John went he looked for young African-American males to mentor and began mentoring Jackie's future husband, a business manager at the local school district. John was a professional at networking and began meeting the school superintendents and attending school functions as part of his interest in helping children.

On March 22, 1988, overriding President Reagan's veto, Congress passed the Civil Rights Restoration Act, which expands the reach of non-discrimination laws within private institutions receiving federal funds. The Act specified that recipients of federal funds must comply with civil rights laws in all areas, not just in particular programs or activities that receive federal funding.

That fall George H. W. Bush was elected President, and Condi was invited to Washington by Scowcroft to work in a one-year fellowship with the Joint Chiefs of Staff, acting as special assistant to the Joint Staff for strategic nuclear policy. She would continue to serve on the Board of Directors for the Mid-Peninsula Urban Coalition and would join and serve for the first time on the Board of Directors for World Politics.

Prior to leaving the security of Stanford to join the Bush Administration, Rice was the Guest of Honor at several campus events. At one such event she was asked how she felt heading into a future that was uncertain.

"Ambiguity has never bothered me at all," she said. "I think that part of it is that I'm pretty religious, and that probably helps to make one less fearful and more optimistic about what's possible."[2]

Condi took an extended leave of absence from Stanford and headed off to Washington, but not before she became a fellow of the Hoover Institution and agreed to serve on the Governor's Independent Advisory Board on Redistricting the State of California.

During her time at the Pentagon and advising the Joint Chiefs of Staff, Condi and President George H. W. Bush quickly bonded, becoming good friends and confidants. During the same time frame, Condi was invited and accepted the offer to be on the Board of Directors for the Social Science Research Council's Committee on Problems and Policy and served on Special Advisory Panels to the Commander-in-Chief of the Strategic Air Command.

After her first year in Washington, D.C. Condi extended her stay and became the senior director of Soviet and East European Affairs in the National Security Council and a special assistant to the President for National Security Affairs. In that role she was responsible for helping develop the strategy of President Bush and then Secretary of State James Baker in favor of German reunification. President Bush was so impressed with her that he introduced her to Soviet leader Mikhail Gorbachev as the one who informed him as to everything he needed to know regarding the Soviet Union.

Despite how busy Condi was with work, she still found time to play the $13,000 Steinway her parents had given her when she was a teen. To continue to feed her soul with the performing arts, she joined the Advisory Board for the Community School for Music and the Arts.

While Condi was in Washington, her father continued to network on behalf of education for youth minorities in California. They visited one another often, and both father and daughter continued to work through the loss of Angelena.

John visited the Ravenswood School District and was talking with the school superintendent when he noticed an attractive black woman in the school office. He asked the superintendent who she was and was introduced to Clara Bailey. She was the principal at Menlo Oaks Performing Arts School in Menlo Park, California. The superintendent left the two alone, and after they talked for a few minutes, they exchanged numbers and soon thereafter began to date.

Ironically, Condi already knew Clara. A few years earlier when she had met Dale Hamel in the spice aisle at Lucky's Supermarket and was asked to play piano at Jerusalem Baptist Church, Clara was a member of the choir. For six months thereafter Condi and Clara would meet with the remainder of the choir on a weekly basis and practice and play for Sunday services. Once John began dating Clara and he introduced her to Condi, they were able to make the connection. Both women were amazed that they'd met previously.

John's health was continuing to deteriorate. He still suffered from gout and diabetes and continued to be overweight. He also had some heart ailments that gave him problems from time to time. Condi encouraged her father over and over to take care of himself and to lose weight and even offered to help him do so, but it was hard since she was living on the other end of the United States.

John missed Condi and longed for the companionship he'd once shared with Angelena. His health continually needed attention, and he wanted desperately to have someone around for support and encouragement. So John and Clara began to talk about getting married. Clara had concerns about marrying John because of his health issues. John was eighteen years her senior and took mass amounts of medications. She feared becoming a widow and grappled with the anguish that would cause her. She loved John, but she also wanted to protect her heart.

After praying and asking the Lord if she should marry John, Clara felt strongly that she should. She knew that the Lord would take care of her no matter what happened. So John and Clara immediately began to plan a wedding a few months down the line. As they did so, John encouraged Clara to marry him immediately and suggested they go to Las Vegas. Without anyone knowing except the two of them, they went to Vegas and got married. They planned to have a ceremony for family and friends in the following months. It wasn't until they visited Condi in Washington, D.C. a month later that they told her they had tied the knot when she was trying to figure out separate sleeping arrangements for the two of them. They eventually had a Christian wedding ceremony in Clara's Palo Alto home. Condi served as the Maid of Honor, and Clara's son Greg from a previous marriage was Best Man.

"John called me from California and told me that he'd met this Christian woman and that they were getting married," remembers friend Annye Marie Downing. "I liked her immediately because she took him into her home and took good care of him. After the wedding he sent me pictures and I teased him, saying, 'You got a woman who looks as close to Ang as you could find.'"

In 1989 Condi joined the Board of Directors for the Carnegie Endowment for International Peace and KQED Public Broadcasting and ended her terms with several other boards.

In February 1989 through March 1991, the period of German reunification and the final days of the Soviet Union, Condi served in the Bush Administration as director and then as senior director of Soviet and East European Affairs at the National Security Council and as special assistant to the President for National Security Affairs in the National Security Council and reported directly to National Security Advisor Brent Scowcroft. In retaining these positions, Condi became the highest-ranking African-American woman ever on the National Security Council.

1989 was an instrumental year for black Americans in government. While Condi was advising President Bush, General Colin Powell became the first black chairman of the Joint Chiefs of Staff, the nation's top military position.

As the principal advisor on the Soviet Union for President Bush, Condi began sitting at the bargaining table during all of the President's meetings with Mikhail Gorbachev, including Gorbachev's visit to the White House.

Condi was well on her way up the ladder, breaking any and all barriers set before her as both an African-American and as a woman. Her knowledge and wisdom regarding the Soviet Union gave her great favor with the President, and when Bush took Gorbachev to Camp David with only a few staff, Condi was one of them, and only one of three women on the trip, along with Mikhail Gorbachev's wife Raisa and Barbara Bush.

In June 1990 President Bush invited Condi to join him in a meeting with Mikhail Gorbachev in San Francisco. As a delegate prepared to talk with Gorbachev, a Secret Service agent protecting him shoved Condi. It was said later that not only had he pushed her, but he singled her out of a receiving line of VIPs for impolite treatment because she was black. He was certain that she shouldn't have been at the event and that her presence there was a mistake. President Bush immediately addressed the situation personally, set the record straight, and insisted that an incident like that should never occur again—and it hasn't.

Condi was a Hoover Institute Fellow and an International Institute at Stanford Senior Fellow and for the first time began consulting on Soviet affairs for ABC News.

The Civil Rights Movement continued to make strides at a steady pace without any major hiccups. In 1991 the Civil Rights

Act reaffirmed affirmative action, continuing to seek to overcome the effects of segregation and other forms of past discrimination in relation to African-Americans and other affected groups from the 1960s. The use of racial quotas as part of affirmative action, however, had led to charges of reverse discrimination in the late 1970s. In the 1980s the federal government's role in affirmative action had been considerably diluted, and in 1989 the Supreme Court had given greater standing to claims of reverse discrimination.

After two years of debates, vetoes, and threatened vetoes, President Bush reversed himself and signed The Civil Rights Act of 1991, strengthening existing civil rights laws and providing for damages in cases of intentional employment discrimination.

That same year United States Senator Pete Wilson had become governor of California. Thus he needed to appoint someone to serve the remainder of his Senate term, and he considered Condi for the job at the prompting of President Bush. But Condi didn't have the political experience that most people have prior to serving in the Senate. Nevertheless he met with Condi, giving her the opportunity to build a political career if that's where she saw her future going. She immediately declined his offer, telling Wilson that she was not interested in running for office. President Bush would not be the last person to see political potential in Condi.

Those years were extraordinary for Condi for many reasons, including serving as an instrumental participant in the fall of the Berlin Wall in 1989. For twenty-eight years the border between East and West Berlin had been closed by an "Iron Curtain" in the form of a wall that served as a barrier between West Germany and East Germany. It had been built during the post-World War II division of Germany in an effort to stop the drain of labor and economic output associated with the daily migration of huge numbers of professionals and skilled workers from East to West Berlin. The barrier was successful, effectively decreasing immigration escapees from two and a half million between 1949 and 1962 to five thousand between 1962 and 1989. However, the creation of the Wall was a propaganda disaster for East Germany and for the Communists as a whole. It became a key symbol of what Western powers regarded as Communist tyranny, particularly after the high-profile shootings of would-be defectors. It was a no-win situation for those seeking democracy.

Political liberalization in the late 1980s, associated with the decline of the Soviet Union, led to relaxed border restrictions in East Germany, culminating in mass demonstrations and the fall of the East German government. On November 9, 1989, the government broadcast a statement allowing the crossing of the border without consequences. East Germans approached and then crossed the Wall by the hundreds and were joined by crowds of West Germans. Together they celebrated the fall of the Iron Curtain. Over the next several weeks the Wall was completely destroyed and instigated German reunification, which formally concluded on October 3, 1990. Partly as a result of German reunification, the Soviet Union collapsed and dissolved into fifteen separate countries.

When the Berlin Wall fell and Germans were joyously flowing across the border, Condi says, she and other aides urged President Bush to go to the scene for the sake of all the Presidents before him who had worked toward this celebrated occasion. President Bush stated that an American President shouldn't interject himself into "the Germans' moment" or rub the Soviets' noses in the West's success.

Condi often looks back at those days when she is stressed or feels like she's in a rut and encourages others to do the same. "If you ever feel bogged down in your routine, or caught in a cul-de-sac, or caught at a dead end," she advises, "just think back to Christmas night in 1991. On that night, the hammer and sickle, the flag of the mighty Soviet empire came down from above the Kremlin for the last time. You will be reminded that no condition, no matter how permanent it seems, is immune to change."[3]

After serving two years on the staff of the United States National Security Council and observing how little the United States understood the 1989-1990 events in Eastern Europe, Condi decided to go back to Stanford and teach. She was fearful that she had grown stale in her role as senior director of Soviet and East European Affairs and was eager to resume her academic career. Furthermore, she missed her dad. They talked every day, sometimes several times a day, but she missed having daily face-to-face contact with him.

During the transition of the Presidency when the Bush Administration was leaving and the Clinton Administration was taking over in the winter of 1993, Strobe Talbott, who directed Russian policy in the Clinton Administration, took President Clinton aside and encouraged him to appoint Condi as ambassador to Moscow. Apparently the incoming President declined to do so for unknown reasons. Condi's offers to be in politics would not cease. There would be more to come in the years to follow.

A professorship in the Political-Science Department was created for Condi at Stanford without the customary national search process, and eyebrows began to be raised in relation to what appeared to be special treatment. While she was grateful for the position, it set a tone of preferentiality for other Stanford faculty who had spent years working and advocating for their positions. That feeling would snowball in the years to come and cause tension in her work environment.

THE TURBULENT YEARS

*S*hortly after making the decision to go back to Stanford and teach, Condi was awarded an honorary doctorate from Morehouse College, the only all-male, historically black, liberal arts college in the United States.

Condi left Washington, went back to Palo Alto, and stayed with her father and his new wife while she got settled once again at Stanford, then bought and moved into a condo on the Stanford campus. Condi and her father enjoyed a renewed intimacy, traveling together to football games and other functions with friends. John had missed his daughter while she was in Washington. After she returned to Palo Alto, John resumed the fatherly role of looking out for her. It is said that on several occasions John would drag his new wife Clara out of bed late at night to go over to Condi's condo at Stanford to make sure she got home okay from a date, being with friends, or work.

As she had done again and again wherever she lived, Condi threw herself into her work and served on several boards in various capacities, including Aspen Strategy Group, Chevron Corporation, Rand Corporation, Hewlett Packard, Transamerica Corporation, Search Committee for the President at Stanford, member of the Governor's Advisory Panel on Redistricting California, consultant to the National Security Council and to ABC News on Soviet affairs, trustee for the National Endowment for the Humanities, and trustee for the Carnegie Corporation of New York.

Condi loved Palo Alto and enjoyed being "home" and around her father and friends again. Stanford brought with it wonderful memories of her first teaching experience, and she was happy to be back teaching.

"Ever since I came to Stanford as a young assistant professor, I have known how fortunate I am to be a part of [that] wonderful place," Condi said upon her return. "But I must say that when I decided to return to the university . . . I did so with even greater commitment to, and appreciation of, the freedom of thought, exploration and expression that the academy allows. There is no other environment that can match the energy of a place like this—where leaders in their fields create ideas and transmit them to the best young minds in the world."[1]

Condi's commitment to affect the young minds in the world did not begin and end at Stanford. Like her father, she had a heart and vision for minority and underprivileged children, specifically those in the area where she lived in Palo Alto, California. Soon thereafter Condi became the vice president of the Boys and Girls Club of the Peninsula.

John had continued to meet with Jackie Glaster, the executive director at the Boys and Girls Club of the Peninsula in Palo Alto, and researched the area and the programs available for minority youth.

"We found out that there were programs already for the kids who were really struggling and not making it at all," remembers Glaster. "There were all kinds of special funding and programs for them, and there were special programs for the really gifted and talented kids, but that middle-ground student who was motivated, had some parental support, but didn't have a lot of funds—there wasn't a lot for them. And that was John's focus, to really help those kids to do what they wanted to do in life, and to help them dream and to realize that they had some goals that they could achieve."

John went to Condi, told her about this specific group of kids, and asked her to help him co-found The Center for a New Generation, a nonprofit organization that would specifically help those middle-ground students in need of financial support and mentorship—and she agreed. Like most nonprofit organizations, they needed a substantial amount of money to get the program up and running. Condi knew exactly whom to call—a woman with enthusiasm for youth and the financial backing to support such a program—Susan Ford.

Ford was a philanthropist who had met Condi in 1991 through her now deceased husband. He had been involved with The Lincoln Club of Northern California, a group that was interested in moderate Republicans, an organization Condi had considered being a member of at one time.

"Condi called me one day," remembers Ford. "She said, 'You know, I really want to do something in a volunteer capacity in this community.' She said she'd been to a graduation in a low-income community and was sort of startled at how much of a big deal they made about graduation. They did that because many of the kids would not go on to finish high school. She was wondering what we could possibly do together."

Ford met with John and Condi and then jumped on the bandwagon and agreed to initially fund the program with their support. The ladies continued to talk about how and where to get the program started. Once they got their nonprofit status and had their program ideas laid out, they needed to find someone to run the program.

"Condi and Susan came to my office one day," remembers Glaster. "I didn't know either of them personally although I knew who they were individually. Susan was a funder for the Boys and Girls Club of which I was the executive director, and I knew Condi through John. They knew I had made great strides with the organization and asked me to be their executive director for The Center for a New Generation.

"I turned them down because I had only been with the Boys and Girls Club for a couple of years, and I had some goals I really wanted to accomplish there. So I told them that I would certainly work with them and help them do everything that they were trying to do because I believed in their project very much."

John and Clara opened their home for meetings, where they would discuss the program outline and demographics. Because of her prestigious position in the community, Condi was able to bring in some heavy hitters for board members, including Larry Triplet, a local businessman who owned several McDonald's restaurants in the community, and he became the Center's treasurer on the Board of Directors.

"I believe The Center for a New Generation was ultimately founded through John's prayer with God and developed that way," says Glaster. "He was a prayer warrior and didn't do anything without praying first. Condi was the same way. She is also very spiritual, and I think a lot of that came from her dad. She was very strong in her beliefs. She prayed very seriously and looked to God for direction and guidance in everything that she did. She always looked to God to help her make the decisions that she would make."

Located in disadvantaged East Palo Alto, the center is an "afterschool academy" for third- to eighth-grade kids who are good students but have no exposure to an enriched curriculum. The kids receive daily tutoring, music instruction, and academic acceleration toward a college track focusing on math, science, language arts, computer literacy, and performing arts. The goal was for the founders, employees, and volunteers to be hands-on, or what they referred to as "minds-on."

"We wanted the kids to really get creative and really get involved in projects," says Glaster. "Not just learning from books, but actually making science and math projects and doing art work so that they were really creatively involved in the education process that was being presented to them. And we wanted it to be very different from the classroom because they were in school all day."

The afterschool program was designed to be fun but rigorous, say its founders. The Center was very specific in the instructors they hired, actually going throughout various school districts to find the cream of the crop, offering them more money than they'd make elsewhere.

"The performing arts division of the program was very big because it was important to John," remembers Glaster. "There was no other music program in the school district at that time, so we started a band. We have so many success stories. One fellow left the program and joined the Marines, and now he's the lead trumpeter for them. We have two other gentlemen who have completed school at Harvard and are now back working at The Center for a New Generation."

One of the major hurdles the board members would have to overcome would be the low expectations the students, parents, and teachers had in regard to their success. "One of these children's teachers once said to me, 'The world you're talking about doesn't exist for my kids. They have no chance in life,'" Condi remembers. "I said, 'I hope that's not what you say to them.'"

In another example a girl in the program approached Condi and asked her if she thought she would succeed. "She was quoting my statistics. She said 65 percent of the kids in her district never finish high school. I said, 'What makes you think you have to be in that 65 percent?'"[2]

John traveled back to Stillman College, which both he and his father had attended, and made special arrangements for students who attended The Center for a New Generation to get college scholarships in order to give the attendees every opportunity to succeed.

Condi remained active as well. "Ever since I've been out of school, most of my efforts outside of work have dealt with trying to give kids an opportunity," says Condi. "I hear 'role model' and I don't mind that, but I'd like to think I could be a role model for some young white males, too. I have never accepted this notion that you have to see somebody who looks like you doing it to make it possible."[3]

Glaster says, "Every year around the holidays we'd have a homecoming dinner, and we'd invite students back who were in high school and college. We'd have them talk to the current students, encourage them, and give them information about what it would take for them to be successful in high school."

John had found his niche and reveled in it, actively working with and mentoring the youth in the program. Enlisting several athletes from Stanford to come and mentor, John was in his element. At about the same time there was a young black man in California who would make headlines for their race, but someone John would never reach or mentor. His name was Rodney Glenn King.

King was thrown into the national spotlight after a brutally violent confrontation with the Los Angeles Police Department (LAPD). The incident was videotaped by a bystander, and it raised a public outcry among viewers who believed it was racially motivated. It was not the first accusation of police brutality against the LAPD but certainly the most substantiated. Almost every raced-based group demanded answers. Supporters of the beating argued that King had a history of crime, but blacks and their sympathizers called foul—his police record should have nothing to do with the race-based beating.

On March 14, 1991 three officers and a sergeant of the LAPD were indicted for "assault by force likely to produce great bodily injury" and for assault "under color of authority." When the four officers charged with using excessive force in subduing King were acquitted on April 29, 1992, by a jury of ten whites, one Latino, and an Asian, it triggered massive rioting in Los Angeles. The riots lasted for three days, making it one of the worst civil disturbances in Los Angeles history. By the time the police and the National Guard restored order, there was nearly one billion dollars of damage, with over fifty people killed, over two thousand injured, and more than eight thousand arrested.

Condi's commitment to her students and the passion she expressed in her subject of political science at Stanford continued and was evident to almost everyone. In 1993 she earned the School of Humanities and Sciences Dean Award for Distinguished Teaching. The honor was given to her in recognition of her distinguished and continuing achievements in original research. Her teaching and research interests included the politics of East-Central Europe and the former Soviet Union, the comparative study of military institutions, and international security policy.

In June 1993 Condi spoke at Class Day for the senior class at Stanford and stated that since the students had come four years prior, the Soviet Union had ceased to exist and Germany had been unified. She encouraged the young adults to "take classes about other cultures, learn languages" and "to study abroad if given the opportunity." She said, "If you've had that chance, the struggles of the peoples of Africa and Asia and Latin America and Europe are your struggles, not because CNN has brought them into your living room, but because your knowledge and experiences have brought you into theirs.

"Everywhere human beings seem determined to outline their differences in blood. They cling to centuries-old myths, some grounded in reality and others not, to fuel their hatred and to pass those hatreds on to successive generations. Throughout history and still here, at the end of the twentieth century, difference is regarded as a license to kill." Such differences include race, sex, and religious beliefs.

The Civil Rights Movement continued to move forward, and Toni Morrison became the first African-American to win the Nobel Prize in Literature.

Condi was a knowledgeable and enthusiastic teacher and was popular among her students. They often saw her in the gym or working out with the Stanford coach and even serving them breakfast in the cafeteria during final exams, a Stanford tradition for teachers.

Within a short time after her return to teaching at Stanford, Condi received an unexpected phone call from the university president, Gerhard Casper. He wanted to talk business with her—in his office. While talking about plans for the school wasn't unusual for the two of them, the meeting officially in his office was.

Casper and Condi had first met when she served on the Search Committee for the university's president in February 1991, when she and some other members of Stanford's presidential search committee visited him in Chicago. Casper had been one of several applicants that she and a group of her colleagues met with and interviewed. Casper was really impressed with Condi from that day on, and after accepting the position he and Condi became good friends.

After she arrived to meet with him, Casper laid his cards out on the table. He wanted her to be the university's provost.

"Condi is not someone who is easily stunned by anything," Casper says, laughing, "but there was absolute silence on the other end of the table."[4]

The duties of Stanford's provost are like those of a chief operating officer in business. If she accepted the position, she would have the responsibility for the internal management of the university. The schools would report to her, and she would oversee the faculty of fourteen hundred, athletics, the $1.5 billion budget, and the academic programs that served fourteen thousand students. It would be the toughest job she'd ever had to date, with a precipitous learning curve and responsibility that far outweighed that of any previous job.

Condi accepted the job, but not without a fight from the university's Provost Search Committee. They had narrowed the list down to a handful of prospective provosts, and Condi wasn't included on the list until Casper personally placed her name there. Then when all of the interviews for the position had been completed, Casper overruled the committee and stated that he wanted Condi in the position. The committee balked. Condi was only thirty-eight and would be the first provost for the school under sixty years of age. Furthermore, she had no previous extensive chairman and managerial experience such as being dean or a department chair and therefore didn't qualify for the job based on Stanford's own guidelines, and she was a Republican (many American universities are made up primarily of Democrats). The Search Committee questioned her ability to do the job, and they encouraged Casper to choose another applicant. As president, Casper had veto power, and he extended it, a bold move for the newly-appointed president. The Search Committee submitted to Casper's request, but this wouldn't be the end of contention in relation to Condi and her new role as provost.

When students got wind of Condi's promotion and the contention it created in the faculty and Search Committee, they opened it up as a topic of discussion in the university newspaper, which only stirred the contention within faculty upper management. Stanford had a history of complaints regarding alleged bias toward minorities and women and blatantly accused Casper of using Condi as a pawn to quiet the accusations. Casper didn't stay silent. Instead he addressed the accusations head-on.

"It would be disingenuous for me to say that the fact that she was a woman, the fact that she was black and the fact that she was young weren't in my mind. They were."[5]

He also said, "Stanford University is most fortunate in persuading someone of Professor Rice's exceptional talents and proven ability in critical situations to take on this task. Everything she has done, she has done well; I have every confidence that she will continue that record as provost. [I am] greatly impressed by her academic values, her intellectual range, and her eloquence. . . . I have come to admire her judgment and persuasiveness as well. In terms of age, Professor Rice will bring into the leadership of the university a generation that

I would like to see play an increasingly important role in Stanford affairs."[6]

Gerald Lieberman, the outgoing provost, supported Casper's decision. "She has tremendous ability and intelligence, and the maturity of someone far beyond her age."[7] When Condi took over the position on September 1, 1993, she was the first African-American, the youngest person, and the first woman to hold the job in the university's 102-year history.

In her acceptance of the position Condi said, "Stanford, like all universities, is a maelstrom of change. Just as I was fortunate to be given a chance to help shape America's response to the extraordinary events that ended the Cold War, I am honored that President Casper has placed faith in my judgment and ability to meet Stanford's challenges. I share his, and the faculty's, love for the academy and strong belief in Stanford. That is why I am so looking forward to joining this team and cherish the chance to work with it and my faculty colleagues in the exciting times ahead."[8]

The treatment of minorities and women had been a long-standing concern for the faculty at Stanford, and there was hope that Condi would be able to quiet the accusatory voices as both a woman and a minority person, but other issues on the table were raging and needed immediate attention. Most importantly, the school's budget was out of control.

Condi was faced with what looked like an insurmountable mountain she had to climb. The 1989 Loma Prieta earthquake and the long-running dispute over federal funds for Stanford research had left Stanford University with a forty-million-dollar deficit, making fiscal discipline difficult at best. Financial scandal threatened to consume the school if the budget weren't brought into balance soon. "I came into a really bad budget situation. I was 38, I'd never even been a department chair, and suddenly I had deans reporting to me who were 20 years older. I had to discipline the university not to spend more than we were taking in and I had to make some very tough calls."[9]

After reviewing the university's records and past attempts to gain control on spending, to many of her colleagues' dismay Condi began slashing tens of millions of dollars from the school budget and discontinued certain programs and departments. Her goal was to have the school solvent within two years, something that her adversaries said was impossible.

"There was a sort of conventional wisdom that said it couldn't be done," remembers Casper, ". . . that [the deficit] was structural, that we just had to live with it. [Condi] said, 'No, we're going to balance the budget in two years.'"[10]

"I am somebody who is very data-driven and analytic," says Condi. "When I see a problem, my first question is, why do we have that problem?"[11]

Condi ran a tight ship as provost and took her role and responsibility seriously. And in doing so she made a few enemies along the way. "Students held a sit-in on the quad, decrying everything I was doing because I had to lay off a very popular administrator."[12] After two long years of getting to work early and staying late crunching numbers, Condi announced that the budget had not only been balanced, but the university was 14.5 million dollars to the good. Her announcement stunned and silenced the pessimists who said it couldn't be done.

"It involved painful decisions, but it worked," recalls Casper. ". . . [it] communicated to funders that Stanford could balance its own books and had the effect of generating additional sources of income for the university . . . it was courageous."[13]

"I'm very proud we are fiscally sound now," Condi announced. "Even after we had already been through $40 million plus of budget rejection under [former provost] Jim Rosse, who had started this process . . . we still had $20 million to go and there wasn't much low-hanging fruit left."[14]

In addressing the treatment of women and minorities, Condi continued to raise eyebrows when she said that she supported special treatment at the time of hiring but not when it came to granting tenure with its promise of prestige, higher pay, and guaranteed job security.

In a controversial meeting of the Faculty Senate Condi said, "I am myself a beneficiary of a Stanford strategy that took affirmative action seriously, that took a risk in taking a young Ph.D. from the University of Denver."

Using herself as an example didn't pacify her accusers. It seemed that no matter what Condi said or did she offended either students, faculty, or both. Condi approached her leadership role with the tools she was taught as a child with her parents—just do what has to be done. Her no-nonsense directness offended many. The once popular and sought after teacher was now somewhat disliked and unpopular among students and faculty. As a result, fifteen professors and Stanford researchers filed a 400-page legal complaint against the university with the U.S. Labor Department, alleging unfair treatment of women and minorities at Stanford. It was a battle that would rage throughout her entire tenure.

Not everyone at Stanford disagreed with Condi's bold moves. Along with the support of Casper, she had friends and colleagues who understood all too well the responsibility of a provost.

"I'm also an administrator," says Lori White, "So I know that our jobs are much more complex than the outside person knows. We are often faced with having to make difficult decisions, so I knew there was much more to this situation than it appeared. If you are a competent and effective administrator, it's likely that not everybody is going to like you, so I was willing to give her the benefit of the doubt.

"Condi was coming from a political environment where most decisions are made unilaterally to an academic environment driven by collegiality. It was a tough transition for her, as it would have been for anyone.

"Condi is a warm person, family-oriented, and she's always trying to figure out ways to get people whom she loves together with one another. People stereotype her as being aloof, or cold, but absolutely none of that is true."

Condi worked hard in her role as provost, going to work early and staying late into the night. The job consumed her. Still, says her family, she remained the same Condi to them—humble, caring, compassionate, and passionate for God, family, and music.

For several years Condi had been driving an old Buick she'd named Boris. After becoming provost, her father and stepmother encouraged her to splurge on herself and buy a new car—specifically a Mercedes. "You can't be provost and drive a beat-up car," her stepmother Clara would tease her lovingly. Finally Condi broke down and bought a Mercedes, getting rid of Boris, a faithful friend throughout the years and a constant reminder of her love for Russia.

Despite the prestigious role and much higher income, Condi's heart remained tender toward the Lord, and he used various circumstances to encourage her in her walk with God and in her dealing with the loss of her mother that continued to ache in her heart. Here is one story that she says greatly impacted her spirit.

"Shortly after I was appointed provost at Stanford University I [heard] a story about how the university originated. Stanford University was founded out of the grief and anguish of two incredible people: Senator Leland Stanford and his wife, Jane. Their son, Leland Stanford, Jr., died at the age of fifteen while traveling in Europe. At that time the Senator and Mrs. Stanford, having lost their only child, decided in their pain that they would do something good for other people's children, so they started the university. It went on to be a successful college, indeed helping to educate thousands of young adults.

"Years later, when Senator Stanford died, the university was, in a real sense, founded a second time. After he passed on, the university faced a dire financial crisis that almost led to its closure. The senator had paid all of the university's expenses personally over the years, and after his death the United States government seized his assets in a dispute over his railroad. The university was suddenly penniless. Jane Stanford's advisors told her that her only choice was to close the university. Instead she rejected that advice and reduced her personal staff from seventeen to three, kept $350 a month out of the ten thousand dollars permitted her by the courts, and placed the faculty on her personal payroll. Over the years thousands of individuals have been able to attain their education because of the sacrifice of these two people in the midst of their personal heartache.

"As I reflect on those acts of faith and courage, first, at the original founding of the university after the death of their son Leland, then again after Senator Stanford died, I realize that Senator and Mrs. Stanford were testament to a belief that we have all but lost in modern life—the conviction that struggle and sorrow are not a license to give way to self-doubt, self-pity, and defeat but rather an opportunity to find a renewed spirit and strength to carry on. Those acts of self-sacrifice in the midst of heartache are perfect examples that today's defeat can be turned into tomorrow's victory.

"As much as we hate to admit it, few of us would have made the same decisions. We live in a world of instant gratification. Our self-centeredness and underlying search for that which makes us feel good today, at whatever the expense and cost tomorrow, is spiritually self-mutilating. Although Christians know that our earthly lives are not yet the final act, we too behave as the ancient Euripideans did, living foolishly for today because tomorrow we might die."[15]

Condi's perspective is profound and piercing to our fragile humanity that screams to be satisfied.

In 1993 as a Chevron board member and stockholder Condi and fifteen members of her family flew to Rio de Janeiro, Brazil where in a launching ceremony she christened an oil tanker that Chevron named after her. The double-hulled giant was part of the international tanker fleet of the San Francisco-based multinational oil firm. The ships were often named after female board members.

During the nights and weekends when Condi was not working late at her Stanford office, she consciously made the effort to spend time with family and friends. It was a time of bonding for Condi and her stepmother Clara who would take turns cooking for the large groups of individuals they entertained. The night often ended with singing from a hymnal with Condi playing the piano.

Many of the Rice gatherings were centered around football. Every Sunday John would invite people over to his and Clara's house to watch a game. He had received a part-time position as a mentor for student athletes at Stanford, so everyone seemed to gather wherever he was. Naturally the Rices would attend all the Stanford games and would often fly out of town for professional games.

"On Sundays Daddy Rice [the nickname those close to John would call him] would invite us over for football, and we'd laugh about who was going to get there first and who was going to get there last," remembers Lori White. "Condi the Presbyterian would get there first, then our friend Randy Bean the Episcopalian would get there second, me, the Methodist, would get there third, and Clara the Baptist would get there last because that's how long our respective church services were. The entire group of us are very faithful and spiritual, but we all worship in different denominations."

White says that Condi's quiet and thoughtful disposition is often misunderstood.

While in California, Condi was approached to run for governor on two separate occasions but declined, saying that she had no interest in running for office. She continued to insist that she wanted to remain at Stanford, and if her role as provost changed, she wanted to do research and teach.

A SEASON OF CHANGE AND LOSS

*C*ondi continued to play the piano, occasionally giving concerts on campus, and became what appeared to be the Stanford Cardinals' number one sports fan. Gathering a group of friends and sometimes family, attending games, and eating out at various restaurants in the towns they traveled to became Condi's entertainment. The evening was often topped off in Condi's hotel room where she and a group of her friends would sing hymns and pray.

Although Condi was the provost at Stanford University, she also continued to teach political science, write dozens of articles for national publications, and author three textbooks.

On February 26, 1993 Arab Islamist terrorists had driven a yellow Ford rental van into the basement of the World Trade Center and set a timer to detonate a 1,500-pound urea-nitrate bomb at 12:17 P.M. The massive blast generated immense pressure and opened a hole almost a hundred feet wide through four sublevels of concrete. The detonation velocity of this bomb was about fifteen thousand feet per second. The cyanide gas generated is assumed to have burned in the explosion, which created a cavernous crater two hundred feet by one hundred feet and seven stories deep in the garage of the World Trade Center. It was intended to devastate the foundation of the North Tower, causing it to collapse onto its twin.

The explosive device did not go off as planned, and the tower did not collapse into the other. Still, the explosion killed six people, injured 1,042, and caused nearly three hundred million dollars in property damage. Had the attack gone as planned, tens of thousands of Americans would have been murdered.

It is said that the terrorists sought to kill Americans for the same reason racists had sought to kill blacks in the civil rights era—because they were different and had different values.[1] Another reason noted by experts is a discrepancy in America's religious beliefs compared to theirs.[2] It was a hate crime motivated by difference.

The attack was planned by a group of militant Islamists and led by Ramzi Yousef, whose uncle was an al-Qaeda member. Eventually the militant Islamists would be captured and held accountable as conspirators and would be convicted for their part in the bombing, each receiving prison sentences of a maximum of 240 years.

During her provost years, Condi continued to attend Menlo Park Presbyterian Church and spoke to various organizations. When she wasn't working or watching football with friends and family, she volunteered at The Center for a New Generation.

Condi had a full but successful plate. Nevertheless, she made time in 1995 to publish her third book, *Germany Unified and Europe Transformed: A Study in Statecraft,* with Phillip Zelikow (Harvard University Press). The comprehensive book is a story of leadership in a crisis, about Germany becoming one nation again after the fall of 1990. The book got rave reviews from experts in the field.

In 1995 she joined the International Advisory Council, and the following year she was an International Affairs Fellow on the Council on Foreign Relations. She also served as the Special Assistant to the Director of the Joint Chiefs of Staff.

In 1997 Condi was appointed by Defense Secretary William Cohen to a special panel that would study the problems of mixed-gender military training and would sit on the Federal Advisory Committee on Gender-Integrated Training in the Military. While retaining her post as provost, Condi was one of nine faculty members at Stanford who have been elected to the American Academy of Arts and Sciences in recognition of her "distinguished contributions to science, scholarship, public affairs and the arts."

She also joined the Board of Directors for the William and Flora Hewlett Foundation and for Notre Dame University, posts she would not hold for long.

Remaining active as she does everywhere she lives, she continued to get up at 5 in the morning and to go immediately to the treadmill to run several miles each day.

In 1998 Condi received a call from Texas governor and Republican presidential candidate George W. Bush. He invited her to Kennebunkport, Maine to talk with him about his campaign and the prospects of a position with his administration should he win the presidential election. When she returned to California she remained tight-lipped about the unexpected meeting.

Later she would say that she respected him from the first time they talked with one another. She is stimulated by his intellect and appreciates the fact that, like her, he cuts straight to the chase. Furthermore, Condi and the then governor had a lot in common. Both love sports including Major League baseball and football, exercise, and politics and have a sarcastic sense of humor and an evangelical faith in God.

The following year Condi joined the Board of Directors of Charles Schwab and began to advise George W. Bush on foreign policy. In doing so, she stepped down as provost of Stanford in June with nothing but praise from the school president Gerhard Casper.

"It's been terrific working with Gerhard," Condi said. "I've enjoyed the job and could happily continue in it. I've decided, though, that it's time to get back to my passion: international relations and politics. I'm going to take a leave from the university to pursue opportunities in the private sector that will give me practical experience in economic and political reform, and in the impact of globalization on international financial and political institutions. I plan to return at some point to teaching and research at Stanford."[3]

Her decision to no longer serve as Stanford's provost surprised no one. She openly shared that the role had been a difficult one, although she far exceeded any of her own or others' expectations and goals. Nonetheless, Casper was at a loss.

"Condi is the best collaborator I've ever had," Casper told the Stanford University News Service. "During the last five years, she has not only been the university provost, but I have treated her as my deputy in every respect. She has fully deserved to be so treated.

"She has been an extraordinarily effective fiscal manager, including making the little-noticed but crucial conversion to a consolidated budget and revenue-constrained budgeting. Together, we have tackled everything from undergraduate education reform to graduate housing.

"The ease with which we have communicated and collaborated is remarkable, given our seeming cultural differences, for instance, in the backgrounds of a black woman from segregated Birmingham, Alabama, and a white man from war-torn Hamburg, Germany. Condi and I have become close friends and substantively disagree primarily about the significance of football."[4]

During her provost tenure, Condi had been courted by other prestigious universities in search for new presidents, but by the time she started to receive offers, she knew enough about the position to know that furthering her career in higher education administration was not the direction she wanted to go.

"I decided I wanted to go back to international politics," Condi said. "You have to make judgments about how long you can afford to be out of your field before you're a dinosaur in it. This is a very fast-moving field and at some point I would be without a place to go back to."[5]

When Condi had first started working as provost at Stanford, she was greatly disliked by many in the administration because of the apparent special treatment she received from Casper and then because of the severe slashing of the budget and the layoffs associated with that. But since that time Condi had worked hard on her image with staff and students by attending several student functions and even addressing the undergraduate class of 1999, where students gave her a standing ovation.

"Looking back she could see how harsh some of her decisions may have seemed, so Condi learned how to soften her approach a bit," says friend Lori White. "She wanted to make sure the students knew that while she had to make tough decisions, she wasn't a tyrant."

In appreciation of her work at Stanford, several farewell parties were organized. At one in particular, a hundred or so African-American students gathered to give Condi their blessing. In an effort to show their love and appreciation, a student sang two of Condi's favorite gospel songs—"I Need Thee Every Hour" and "His Eye Is on the Sparrow." Condi cried at the show of affection.

Over the six years that Condi was provost, the students and faculty had stepped back from their initial full-frontal attack. It had been at least four years since her ability to do the job had been questioned.

Condi had given her notice as provost but also took a leave of absence as a political science professor. However, knowing she'd be back at Stanford someday, she didn't put her campus condominium up for sale or sell her sports tickets for any Cardinals athletics.

For the next seventeen months Condi was on and off the campaign trail with presidential candidate George W. Bush, advising him on foreign policy, helping him with speeches, and even typing them herself when necessary. She continued to do some work for J.P. Morgan on international economic issues but slowly but surely stepped down from other commitments.

As she rode the campaign trail, she and George W. Bush became even better friends. For Condi, one of the greatest blessings was that among the many things they had in common was a clear faith in God.

"Among American leadership, there are an awful lot of people who travel in faith. It's a remarkable thing and I think it probably sets us apart from most developed countries where it is not something that is appreciated quite as much in most of the world."[6]

In February 2000 Condi received a phone call from her stepmother, Clara. Condi's father, John, had suffered a severe attack of arrhythmia and was in the hospital.

John had been giving an interview to a reporter about Condi when his head dropped and his body slumped down suddenly. The interviewer asked if he was okay, and John raised his head long enough to ask them to call his wife. The reporter wisely called 911 first.

According to Clara, John had been so busy caring for other people that he had neglected to get his heart medication filled. As a result his heart's irregular beating took its toll and began to stop working, leaving John in an Intensive Care Unit in a California hospital.

Condi immediately joined Clara by John's side. The doctors told Condi and Clara that the attack was so severe that John's mind was not his own and advised them to take him off life support and let him die. Clara fought the advice.

"'John loved life,' I told Condi. 'He'd want to live.' I told her that we should wait and see what God did. So she said okay, and we began to pray. We did end up taking him off life support, and surprisingly he did well. His vital signs got better, and after a couple of days he opened his eyes."

Even though John continued to have what appeared to be coma-like symptoms, Clara and Condi celebrated and continued to sit by his side in the hospital and prayed even more. After the third day a miracle occurred.

"He looked like he wanted to say something but was struggling," remembers Clara. "Condi and I just watched as tears fell down our faces. Then it happened—the first thing to come out of his mouth after almost dying was the song 'In the Garden.' He started singing, 'I come to the garden alone, while the dew is still on the roses,' and Condi and I joined in. The most amazing thing is that after the first verse and the chorus were sung, Condi and I quit singing because we didn't know all the words, but John just kept on singing by himself until the song was over."

The doctors moved John out of the Intensive Care Unit and into a regular hospital bed, and for days on end Condi and Clara would sing various hymns with him. Ironically, although he could sing praise songs, he was frail and had difficulty speaking complete sentences and having prolonged conversations. Friends came by in droves to visit the much-loved mentor.

"When John got sick I would visit him in the hospital," says Glaster, the president of the Boys and Girls Club of the Peninsula in Palo Alto. "When I was there, Condi would be there singing to her father with Clara. His favorite song was, 'In the Garden.' John would sing that song again and again, and then Condi and Clara would harmonize it beautifully. Then they would pray together."

John was later transferred to a rehabilitation home. After he was settled in, Clara went back to work full-time as the principal of Menlo Oaks Performing Arts School and would visit and spend time with him after work and on the weekends. Condi visited and called daily, if not several times a day, to check on her father and often flew back to Palo Alto to visit him.

John was eager to go home, so Condi and Clara immediately got a hospital bed and had it moved into John and Clara's home. Then Condi hired a team of qualified hospital caretakers to care for her father around the clock, paying for his care out of her own pocket. John was ecstatic to come home, and his two girls did everything they could to make his life as comfortable and as normal as possible.

"They brought him home, and we had a birthday party for him," remembers Glaster. "He loved music, and they had a combo there playing religious music along with mellow secular music with a singer."

Condi continued to travel on the campaign trail with Governor Bush, and Clara went back to work at the school. Due to John's health, Clara put in for early retirement and was waiting for it to go through so she could be home with John all the time.

During meals John wanted to eat with Clara in the dining room. One day when Clara's son Greg was visiting and they were all around the table getting ready to eat, Clara asked Greg to pray over the food. Suddenly John started praying. Clara and Greg looked at one another in grateful surprise.

Friends say that George Bush had already talked with Condi about being his National Security Advisor when he was campaigning, and that caused a conflict within her heart.

After a heated election between George W. Bush and former Vice President Al Gore, Bush won the vote. He immediately appointed Condi as the National Security Advisor on December 18, 2000. In doing so, she became the first woman and only African-American to hold the post since it was created by President Dwight Eisenhower in 1953. As her father watched the announcement from his hospital bed at home, tears welled up in his eyes and ran down his face. Angelena hadn't been able to see their daughter's vast success, but he had, and he was proud.

After President Bush's announcement Condi flew home to Palo Alto to be by her father's side. As she helped Clara care for her father, she wondered how she'd be able to leave him in his deteriorating condition and move to Washington.

Three days later, after Condi had left John and Clara's and headed for her condo at Stanford, John's evening aide got him settled into bed. Feeling confident that all was well, Clara went into her bedroom to sleep. As soon as she shut her bedroom door John suffered another attack of arrhythmia and was once again placed on life support in the Intensive Care Unit.

Condi was immediately at her father's side. This time doctors took a scan of John's brain and showed it to both women. It indicated that the John they knew was no longer there—he had suffered severe and permanent brain damage and would never recover. He was taken off life support, and three days later, on Christmas Eve, John Rice passed from this life.

"We all believe Daddy Rice gave his daughter a wonderful gift by going on to the other side when he did," says Lori White. "He was very conflicted about her being National Security Advisor." John feared for his daughter's safety.

The tears rolled down many faces at John's funeral, but none of them fell from his daughter's eyes. Instead, Condi sang his favorite hymns from the stage, then personally greeted every guest. Attendees say she was calm and serene. Just as she had experienced when her mother had died about fifteen years earlier, she knew that while her father's death hurt now, it had no sting eternally. Her father had accepted Jesus Christ as his Savior, and according to her faith in God, she knew she'd see him again someday in heaven. Undoubtedly she grieved as anyone would after the death of a parent although she remained calm at his funeral.

"Her father's death was very difficult for her," remembers White. "She's not typically an emotional person, meaning that she doesn't wear her emotions on her sleeve, but it was a time when I saw her more emotionally expressive than I'd seen in a long time. I know that was a very difficult time for her to say good-bye to her father with whom she was very, very close and at the same time realize the enormity of taking on this position as National Security Advisor. I mean, this was all happening at the same time, so it was a challenging time for her. But going back to her deep and abiding faith, I know that she believed that God was leading her in this new direction and that he was going to provide her with whatever she needed to be able to move on to the next phase of her life. Also, leaving Clara behind to grieve was something she thought about. I don't think either Clara or Daddy [Rice] would have wanted Condi to stay there because they knew that she had a purpose in the world, that the Lord was calling her to a different place now."

A conflict of emotion stirred in the nation's new National

Security Advisor. On one hand she was ecstatic about the new position in the Bush Administration. Her future on the horizon of life indicated great things, but at the same time life had ended for her in another way. Still, friends say that God had been working long before this day to nudge Condi in the right direction.

"Condi had been traveling with the campaign for President Bush, so she was back and forth a lot, coming home to see her dad before he died," says White. "Bush had already asked her to be National Security Advisor, and it would have been very difficult to accept the position as National Security Advisor while her father was so ill and she'd be in Washington, D.C. and would not have been able to be there to see him every day. We talk about how the Lord works in mysterious ways. I don't know if somewhere in Daddy's [Daddy Rice's] consciousness he understood that this was something that she was wrestling with and may have made the decision that, 'Okay, it's time for me to move on so I can let my daughter go and do what it is that she needs to do.' [Condi and I] often wonder about that."

Condi's father's death left her an adult orphan with parental direction, guidance, and security permanently removed. It stole the person who cared for her more than anyone else ever could and inevitably brought the loss of all ties to her childhood. Her two most trusted confidants and teachers were now both gone, and there would never be a person she'd grow to be that close with again.

Condi immediately filled out the paperwork necessary to have her mother's remains transported from Denver to Palo Alto so she could bury her parents together in California. As she moved into her new position of leadership for the United States, Condi says she learned some important lessons in regard to mourning her loss.

"I learned three important truths while grieving the loss of my parents," Condi says. "First, I feel impressed to say that it is a privilege to struggle. Only through struggle do we realize the depth of our resilience and understand that the hardest of blows can be survived. Through struggle we learn to let go of fear and strive for freedom. Only in struggle do we attain the knowledge that, like a house of cards, the human spirit is fragile and human strength fleeting.

"As [Christians], we can take unique advantage of this truth because in times of despair we can seek a closer relationship with our Lord. How else are we to get to know the full measure of the Lord's capacity for intervention in our lives? If there are no burdens, how can we know that he will be there to lift them?

"It is easy to thank God when all is going well. It is much harder to trust him in times of trial. I think that this is an especially hard lesson, an especially hard belief for those of us who have relied on education, intellect, and reason to guide us. We get sidetracked sometimes and begin to believe that our own wisdom guides us. The media doesn't help. Every single day they bombard us with messages that tell us we can only believe that which we can prove.

"I have had to live my life in the world of the mind because of my career choices. I spend every waking day dedicated to the search to know truth. I am surrounded in my life by standards of evidence and methods of proof. It is sometimes hard to accept the simple faith required to trust in God opposed to my own wisdom.

"The Lord gave us a brain, and I'm quite sure that he expects us to use it, though I'm sure he must be mightily disappointed sometimes. In doing so, there will be times that we wrestle with our faith, questioning and trying to understand God. I have never believed that God intended us to leave the powers of reason aside when we encounter questions of theology or seeming contradictions in our belief, or even when we have questions to ask him. But there are times when intellect and reason fail, when the burden is just too heavy, when it just makes no sense. Those are moments in life that we can't explain what's happening to us, and we must turn to God to be comforted.

"Church, God, and Christianity were like breathing in my family. And while I grew up being certain in my religious faith, it is easy for me to go on spiritual autopilot. If I'm not careful, my faith in Christ can become as habitual as putting on a sweater or eating breakfast in the morning. As a response, my intellect often gets in the way of my faith.

"A couple of years ago I attended the memorial service for a nineteen-year-old Stanford student who was killed in a car accident. I was struck by the fact that the mourners who attended her memorial were so young. It should be decades before they have to go to a funeral for one of their peers. It makes no sense to ask why. There aren't any answers. At those times the relationship that we have developed with God, having trusted him in times of struggle, is the key to our survival. That is when it is time just to give up and turn to God. That is when it is time to let go and take everything to God in prayer. We have a reliable friend to help us through, one who sticks closer than a brother.

"The apostle Paul affirmed this more beautifully than any before him or any since. Locked in prison, Paul warned off those who would feel sorry for him. To the Philippians, Paul wrote, 'I have learned in whatever state I am, to be content. I know how to be abased, and I know how to abound. Everywhere and in all things I have learned both to be full and to be hungry, both to abound and to suffer need.' As Paul taught in this brilliant passage, finding peace in the midst of pain is the fulfillment of one's humility, and the relationship with God is complete.

"There's a second truth about struggle: it can conquer you, or you can conquer it. We are all in a constant search of heroes. This is because they are people who remind us that we can beat the odds. Whether it's Joe Montana helping bring a team back from insurmountable odds as he did multiple times in his career, or Dan Jansen, the speed skater in the Winter Olympics who disappointed America twice in Olympic competition and still found the will to train four more years and ultimately to win a Gold Medal, we keep looking for people who can show us how to triumph over what may appear to be insurmountable circumstances. When other people rise above their circumstances, we feel empowered to do the same. The core attitude of a hero is found in the way that he or she meets life's challenges.

"Part of not allowing struggle to overcome our faith is attained by letting go of our own expectations and plans. Women are used to handling households, raising children, meeting the needs of their mate, and often while working full-time outside the home. Things generally run smoothly for women when they control the circumstances around them. They've set the schedule and the time line for the events that occur from meals to homework to transportation. They are experts at listening and figuring out the cues of the people in their life and moving them in the direction needed to accomplish the goals of the family.

"Women are used to handling difficult circumstances daily in a methodical, calculated manner. It takes a lot of faith to step back from that approach and let go when we need to grieve or work through any type of struggle.

"There is a third truth in the privilege of struggle. You can find personal fulfillment and peace in times of pain and heartache. Difficulties are necessary to hone the spirit and to make us aware of the power not only to survive but to overcome. It is an even greater gift to be able to turn one's sorrow to the good and benefit of others.

"Consider again Jane Stanford, the powerful woman of God, whose faith was tested and purified with the death of her son, and then later, her husband. She is later quoted as saying:

"'My dear husband was suddenly and unexpectedly called from earth to the fair beyond. For a while, I felt like one on a sinking ship on a tempestuous sea. I shuddered and closed my eyes as I thought the ship would sink but clung to God's promises to the helpless, the widow, the weary who wanted rest. I wanted to join my loved ones and was not afraid to die.

"'Suddenly there loomed out before me, the blessed work left to my care by my loved ones, and I felt that my course was cowardly. I was so impressed by the new light that dawned over me it brought the first tears to my eyes. I wept day and night in penitence. I had forgotten God, Jesus Christ, and the angel world that held all that was dearest and best to me. They all said, live—take care of your body—it is the only instrument given you to do the will of the Lord. I promised most solemnly to live for the work that I now saw was God's work, not mine. I promised most solemnly to live for that work and to do my best.'

"In 1904, Jane Stanford said, 'I could see a hundred years ahead when all the present trials were forgotten, and all the present active parties gone—I could see the children's children's children coming here from the East, the West, the North, and the South.'" Mrs. Stanford could not have known that students would come not just from those parts of the United States but from the east, west, north, and south of the globe. She could not have known how crucial it would be to the twenty-first century for people from the corners of the earth to find a place to seek common ground.

"From the great depths of her sorrow, Mrs. Stanford went on to save Stanford University for other people's children. Few of us are offered such dramatic and profound opportunities to do good for others out of our personal struggle. But just as Jane Lathrop Stanford awoke from the depths of her self-pity to a renewed spirit and strength, there are times in our lives when we are called to do the same.

"Today when every person, every group, every nation seems determined to dwell on that which has not been given to us and to point constantly to that which has been given to others, we are badly in need of the power of this lesson. Nothing good is born of personal struggle if it is used to fuel one's sense of entitlement or superiority to those who in our own perception have struggled less than we.

"I've often wondered if Mrs. Stanford's decision to somehow sustain Stanford University was a decision of a grieving widow and mother who wanted to continue to immortalize her son and her husband. But it is clear to me from her response that she in fact saw a higher calling. She understood the link between her own pain and suffering and her calling to God.

"Few of us are presented with so many dramatic opportunities to demonstrate that struggle can be for the good. But there are times in our lives when we are called to rise above our pain and to help others. In today's society every person, group, and state seems determined to dwell on that which has not been given to us and to point constantly to that which has been given to others. It is a dangerous thing to ask why you have been given less than someone. It is humbling and healthy to ask why you have been given so much.

"Struggle is not to be worn as a badge of honor. Struggle can only be turned to the good of others if we can let go of the pain, bad memories, and the sense of unfairness of the 'Why me' that inevitably accompanies personal turmoil.

"We as Christians need to reaffirm for our troubled world that struggle is a privilege. The human condition contains one central paradox, one that philosophers, religious leaders, and people of letters have tried to explain through the centuries. It is a lesson that is at the root of Christianity, at the basis of our belief in the resurrection. It was revealed to us at the founding of our faith in the most dramatic way possible. It is that our Lord Jesus Christ suffered a horrible death only to rise again. There was Good Friday, but there was also Easter Sunday.

"The paradox of the human condition then is this: in death we find life; in turmoil we find peace; one must lose one's life to gain it; and in struggle we find that which is irrepressible in the human spirit and always there in our relationship with God. The affirmation of that paradox of the human condition, a belief in the privilege of struggle, is heard in the words of a Negro spiritual.

"In the most horrendous conditions, when it must have seemed that there was no way out, nowhere to go, slaves raised their voices in the song 'Nobody Knows the Trouble I've Seen.' From the depth of their pain, they knew that although others may not understand their heartache, Jesus did. As they sang, 'Nobody knows the trouble

I've seen; nobody knows but Jesus. Nobody knows the trouble I've seen, Glory Hallelujah. Sometimes I'm up, sometimes I'm down. Yes, Lord, You know sometimes I'm almost to the ground. Nobody knows the trouble I've seen, nobody knows but Jesus,' they knew they spoke from the power of the resurrection.

"I often wonder how completely the church understands suffering and the context of joyful hand-clapping and dancing that is found in black gospel. Gospel was born in the small, hot, black churches where the people who were celebrating were, oddly enough, those who had nothing to celebrate in this earthly life. The joyful celebration came from the depths of despair. The church was the one place they could express joy. Black gospel is directly tied to the pain and suffering that was the legacy of slavery and segregation. The context needs to be understood, that there is a link between joy and pain, faith and perseverance, and struggle and salvation.

"Again the words of the apostle Paul are relevant: 'I was given a painful wound to my pride, which came as Satan's messenger to bruise me. Three times I begged God to rid me of it, but God's answer was: 'My grace is sufficient for you, for my power is made perfect in weakness' (2 Cor. 12:7-10). Therefore I shall prefer to find my joy and my pride in the things that are my weakness; and then the power of Christ will come and rest upon me. For this reason I am content, for the sake of Christ, with weakness, contempt, persecution, hardship, and frustration; for when I am weak, then I am strong.

"Once again, it is a privilege to struggle. When God's power is full-strength because we are weak, that enables the Spirit of the Lord to rest on us, and it is indeed a great day in the Lord. When, for the sake of Christ, we are weak, contemptible, persecuted, frustrated, and painfully grieving, because we are weak, he is strong, and it is a blessed day in the Lord.

"As Christians, we sometimes take for granted God's intricate plan for our lives. I have had my struggles, as perhaps you have, but frankly, when I look at what other people have confronted on a daily basis, like what my parents and grandparents dealt with, I am reminded that I have hardly lived the life of Job. And with that grace and support from God I have come to terms with every day.

"Only through struggle can we realize the depth of our resilience and understand that in the darkest of nights we can let go of fear and rest in the freedom of the shadow of the Lord who suffered all things for us. It is only through struggle that we can truly understand the truth of rejoicing in suffering, found in Romans 5:3, 'Not only so, but we also rejoice in our sufferings, because we know that suffering produces perseverance.'"[7]

From the Inside Looking Out

On January 15, 2001 Condi resigned from being head of the Chevron Committee on Public Policy to become National Security Advisor. As an advisor to the President, Condi's new job was to faithfully represent the views of the different agencies that make up the National Security Council and to organize the decision-making process so that the President could come to a decision. Critics said that the oil tanker that Chevron had named after her in Brazil in 1993 now posed serious diplomatic and ethical issues for Condi and the administration, and therefore the name needed to be changed. Many rolled their eyes in disbelief that the issue was even brought up, but Condi agreed to have her name removed, and Chevron renamed the oil tanker *Altair Voyager*.

Washington insiders watched Condi like a hawk, wondering if she was in over her head as National Security Advisor. They'd have their answer soon enough. Less than three months after being sworn in for her new job United States officials reported that a U.S. Navy electronic surveillance aircraft that had been on a routine mission over international waters off China was involved in a collision and had to make an emergency landing on China's Hainan Island, about four hundred miles southwest of Hong Kong.

The Chinese government would not release the crew of twenty-four or the plane, which was loaded with sensitive intelligence-gathering equipment. In response Condi promptly assisted the President by formulating an approach for the potentially explosive negotiations, and it worked, giving Condi a few nods of approval from even the highest pedestals in Washington.

Condi went on to advise the President in other sensitive circumstances such as the Anti-Ballistic Missile Treaty with Russia. As a result Condi had to stay prepared for just about anything that might threaten our nation's security. Then something happened to Condi that came from out of nowhere, blindsiding her and bringing her to her proverbial spiritual knees.

"I had gone to the doctor for a checkup when, during my breast exam, my doctor found something unusual," Condi recalls. "My mother died from breast cancer, so this was not good news. My doctor said something like, 'Well, don't worry, it's early. Whatever it is, it's early.' Believe me I was less worried about how early it was than what it was. But the doctor said he didn't know and wouldn't know for about a week. That was one of the longest seven-day periods of my life.

"During the first few days after meeting with my doctor, I found myself planning my future. How was this illness going to interfere with my life? How was I going to keep working if I had cancer? I started planning whom I would tell and whom I wouldn't. I had a schedule all laid out *if* indeed I did have breast cancer. One night toward the end of my seven-day waiting period, I woke up in the wee hours of the morning and thought, *Have you lost your mind?* I realized that I was attempting to control a circumstance that I had no control over. So I changed the way I had been praying.

"I started by asking God to take control of the situation. That meant that I had to let go of it. Additionally, I began to ask him how this experience could teach me about what I really should be doing with my life and to show me what I wasn't getting done in my life. I made the radical break between faith and reason, letting go of my expectations and plans and allowing God to take them. I thank the

Lord that I didn't end up having cancer but was also thankful for the lesson I learned in the process of finding out.

"[Then] I realized the importance of taking the time to grapple with my circumstance in his presence. I needed time for silence, reflection, and meditation. I had to make time to sit and be still so that I could hear the still, small voice of calm that doesn't come when I'm allowing my intellect and reason to dominate every waking moment."[1]

God used the breast cancer scare to draw Condi to a place where she was dependent upon him as opposed to relying on her intellect and ability to reason, the same lesson she had grappled with and overcome in relation to her parents' deaths. Little did she know that the Lord was preparing her for an even bigger trial in the distant future.

Condi loved working in the White House. "You walk into the Oval Office, all that history, you realize that Roosevelt was there and Kennedy was there, and you realize what the office means because America's really an extraordinary place," she said. "And around the world, America is revered for its love of freedom, for its willingness to be generous with other people, and we try to embody that in our foreign policy. We try to remember that America stands for more than power. It stands for ideals and this president has spent a lot of time talking about making the world safer but also making the world better. And that's what the Oval Office stands for."[2]

Equally so, she loved working alongside President Bush. They spent a lot of time together, and she adored his sense of humor. She also had nothing but great things to say about his character and his faith in God. The great respect and admiration she had for him she also received from her own aides.

Those who know her best behind the secured building of the White House have two nicknames for her—both conveying respect and affection. Some refer to her as the "anti-Kissinger" because, unlike Henry Kissinger, she is humble and does not have the driving need to show her authority or power. Other refer to her as "Warrior

Princess" because of her role and faith in God and the fact that she handles her job with steel-like precision and presence.

THE DAY THE WHOLE WORLD CRIED

On September 11, 2001 Condi had gotten out of bed at 5 in the morning, just like she does every day of the week, and immediately went to the treadmill to begin her daily run. It had been a part of her morning routine for years, listening to music or catching up on the news while exercising. "I do some of my best thinking on the treadmill," she says. "Exercise is a very high priority for me."[3]

After running, she ate a bowl of cereal, showered, got dressed, and with her Secret Service men in tow climbed into her chauffeured vehicle and went to work at the White House.

One of the first things she did after she passed by the President's office, which is only a few feet away from her own, was to get a briefing on the morning's events and relative information regarding intelligence. Nothing out of the ordinary had been reported regarding the United States in the few hours that she had slept. Then around 9 in the morning it happened.

Condi's executive assistant approached her and told her that a jet airliner had crashed into one of the two towers of the World Trade Center in New York City. Condi's first impression was that it was an accident, and she asked the reporting aide to keep her posted on how many casualties there were and any other relative information. She then called the President who was in Florida. After that she went to a staff meeting. In the middle of the meeting, Condi's executive assistant approached her again with a note that said that a second plane had hit the World Trade Center. That's when she knew it was a terrorist attack.

Condi immediately ended the meeting, went into the Situation Room of the White House, and began to gather the National Security Council principals for an emergency meeting, including Colin Powell and Donald Rumsfeld. As she did so, someone came up to her and told her to get to the bunker and that the Vice President was already there.

Condi called President Bush to talk about whether or not he should come back since it was obvious that Washington was under fire.

Once she got to the bunker she called her aunt and uncle in Birmingham to tell them she was okay, then began to call other governments to make sure they knew that the United States government was up and running.

That September 11 morning, nineteen terrorists affiliated with al-Qaeda hijacked four commercial passenger jet airliners. After United Airlines Flight 175 and American Airlines Flight 11 crashed into the World Trade Center, both towers collapsed within two hours. American Airlines Flight 77 flew into the Pentagon in Arlington County, Virginia. Passengers and flight crew members on a fourth aircraft, United Airlines Flight 93, attempted to retake control of their plane from the hijackers and in doing so crashed into a field in rural Somerset County, Pennsylvania. After the events of the day had taken their toll, almost three thousand Americans' lives had been taken by that international hate crime.

On the evening of 9-11 Condi had great difficulty sleeping. "I probably woke up every thirty minutes or so," remembers Condi.[4]

Condi was immediately thrown into the public eye as America grappled to pick up the pieces of the horrific events of that day. To Americans Condi said, "We have been reminded in dramatic and terrifying ways of what happens when difference becomes a license to kill. Terrorism is meant to dehumanize and divide . . . memories of the Birmingham bombing have flooded back to me since September 11." Rumors about U.S. intelligence knowing of the attacks prior to their occurring turned into accusations intertwined with a blanket of mourning that covered one end of the world to the other.

In an attempt to do damage control, Condi spoke on the Arab language TV network Al Jazeera to counter statements by al-Qaeda that America hates Muslims. As more attacks against America and her people were threatened, the National Security offices buckled down on security in every arena. Now in a defensive position from the brutal and relentless attack, it would take years for America to get back to where she was before the assault—if she ever really would at all.

Condi slept little in the days and weeks that followed. She was responsible for protecting the United States from external intruders, all the while doing the same internally. Along with other day-to-day requirements, doing her job as National Security Advisor was taxing to say the least.

Condi says that whenever she feels overwhelmed she prays a lot. And when she needs "guidance and strength of conviction" she often reads Romans 5, which in part says, "we rejoice in our sufferings, knowing that suffering produces endurance, and endurance produces character, and character produces hope, and hope does not put us to shame, because God's love has been poured into our hearts."

She says she relies on the wisdom of friends and family. "I have very good friends in foreign policy who are just very, very smart. . . . I also have two or three really close friends from my time at Stanford whom I talk to all the time. I try to draw on the wisdom of the American people through my relatives. . . . And then, I'm a deeply religious person, so I turn to prayer frequently."[5]

President Bush put Condi in charge of defending the administration against accusations that they failed to act on intelligence, which critics said could have prevented the tragedy. Despite the onslaught of attacks against the administration and the lack of faith in her as National Security Advisor, Condi stayed focused, self-composed, and strong. She says that the strength we see in her is not her own but belongs to the God she serves.

As America waited for direction from the National Security Advisor, asking "Why?" and "How?" again and again, Condi prayed. What would happen next? How would America recover? Who was responsible? What was the United States willing to do about it? Is anyone safe? How can we protect ourselves now? Citizens of the United States watched their televisions anxiously, awaiting the answers.

As in the death of both her parents, Condi had to desperately cling to her faith in God during that time. She had no one to run to for emotional shelter, no one to encourage her when she grew tired, and no one to help her on the worst day of America's life—no one, that is, but God.

"When you go through something like that, you have to turn to faith because you can rationalize it, you can make an intellectual answer about it, but you can't fully accept it until you can feel it here [taps chest]. That time wasn't a failure, but it was a period of crisis when faith was really important for me."[6]

"I think after 9/11, we all needed our faith very, very strongly. I remember immediately after, there wasn't much left except to pray. And again, I remember Abraham Lincoln saying that sometimes you have to get on your knees, because your intellect won't fully explain. And regardless of the circumstance, my faith has always come through for me."[7]

Condi combated an array of emotions during this time, including self-examination. "In this job, when we faced a horrible crisis like September 11th, you go back in your mind and think, 'Is there anything I could have done? Might I have seen this coming? Was there some way?'"[8]

As she worked through her own pain from the unexpected tragedy and from her father's death less than a year earlier, she had to do whatever she could to protect and strengthen America's weak spots in the event of another attack. As bodies were being found in droves, Condi tried to console a weeping nation, all the while grappling with her own grief. She went on to help fortify America's ports of entry and put together a plan and advocate for a war that would help bring an end to the fear of terrorist attacks.

"I think as a country we're adjusting to the fact that we are vulnerable. We're doing everything that we can to minimize those vulnerabilities on a daily basis, but we're also on the offense. We're not going to stand back and wait for the terrorists to come to us. We're going to go out and hunt them down and make certain that over time America is more secure and that what happened to us on September 11th can't happen again."[9]

Condi prayed again and again over her crucial decisions, and many faith-based believers around the world believed that God had put her in the position she was in for such a time as this. If God had called her to be our country's security leader, he would certainly equip her to do the job if she chose to cling to him.

Lori White explains how Condi pushes through difficult times. "Condi has been able to manage her increasingly complex life in an increasingly complex world. I think understanding her faith is the key to that. She's one of the most calm people that I know, and the reason is because she fundamentally believes that given all of the information she has available to her on any given day, and given her faith, God is going to allow her to make the best decision possible given the information that she has available to her, to be able to manage the job she has and to be calm, level-headed, [and] polite to people even in the midst of protesting or angry questions. I don't think anybody has really ever seen her lose her cool. She understands that the decisions that she makes in conjunction with President Bush and his administration are going to affect people for years to come, and all that weighs on her mind. But again, it is her faith in God and his guiding her to make the best decisions possible given the information that she has that keeps her going, and that's [why] she's able to sleep well at night."

Condi agrees with White's overall view of her faith and spiritual role in life. "I try always to not think I am Elijah, that I have some-how been particularly called. That's a dangerous thing," Condi says. "In a sense, we've all been [called] to whatever it is we are doing. But if you try to wear the imprimatur of God—I've seen that hap-pen to leaders who begin too much to believe . . . I try to say in my prayers, 'Help me to walk in your way, not my own.' Try to walk in a way that is actually trying to fulfill a plan, and recognize you are a cog in a larger universe."[10]

At the same time, when she questions circumstances in her life and those in the lives of others, she does see that God is in control and that the future is bright, regardless of what current circumstances indicate.

"I feel that faith allows me to have a kind of optimism about the future. You look around you, and you see an awful lot of pain and suffering and things that are going wrong. It could be oppressive. But when I look at my own story or many others that I have seen, I think, 'How could it possibly be that it has turned out this way?' Then my only answer is, it's God's plan. And that makes me very optimistic that this is all working out in a proper way if we all stay close to God and pray and follow in his footsteps. I really do believe that God will never let you fall too far. There is an old gospel hymn [that says], 'He knows how much you can bear.' I really do believe that."[11]

Condi became the most visible member of President George W. Bush's Cabinet, and she quickly became the face of the White House as she was continually interviewed by media outlets. With that high-profile position came the responsibility and opportunity to share how she retained her strength. In a speech on the National Day of Prayer Condi stated that while other people gather strength from a variety of sources, she gets hers from one central place.

"For me it comes from a deep and abiding faith in Jesus Christ. Since I was a little girl, I have relied on faith—a belief that I'm never alone, that the bottom will never fall out too far. That has always been a part of me, and I'm drawing on that now. I'm not a worrier. When I'm concerned about something, I figure out a plan of action, and then I give it to God. I just ask him to carry me through it. God's never failed me yet."[12]

In their sympathy for the families who lost loved ones in the 9/11 tragedy, President Bush, First Lady Laura Bush, and Condi met and talked with and wrote letters to encourage them as they grieved.

"The families . . . have heard from this President . . . and from me, personally, in some cases, how deeply sorry everyone is for the loss that they endured. You couldn't be human and not feel the horror of that day."[13]

Condi and her team worked hard over the next several months to bring safety in homeland security to fortify America against terrorists. They knew it would take time, and as the process continued she said Americans were getting safer and safer.

In a commencement address she gave to Stanford students after 9/11, Condi shared how the events of that tragic day brought back the terror of the attack against blacks early in her life in Birmingham.

"In the months past, we have been reminded in dramatic and terrifying ways of what happens when difference becomes a license to kill," she shared. "Terrorism is meant to dehumanize and divide. Growing up in Birmingham, Alabama, I saw the home-grown terrorism of that era. The 1963 bombing of the 16th Street Baptist Church was meant to suck hope out of the future by showing that hope could be killed—child by child. My neighborhood friend, Denise McNair, was killed in that bombing, and though I didn't see it, I heard it a few blocks away. And it's a sound that I can still hear today.

"Those memories of the Birmingham bombing have flooded back to me since September 11, and as I watched the conviction of the last conspirator in the church bombing last month, I realize now that it is an experience that I have overcome but will never forget."

As 2002 revealed itself in the wake of the tragedy of 9/11, Condi was nominated and received a NAACP Image Award at a ceremony in Los Angeles, California. Although the award is historically given primarily to entertainers, the NAACP also recognizes people who have advanced the cause of minorities through leadership or example. As NAACP President Kweisi Mfume bestowed the group's President Award on Condi, he praised her for becoming the first woman to be appointed as National Security Advisor and gave her due credit for overcoming bias against women and Africans in her career.

On April 22, 2002 Condi was given the opportunity to perform with Yo-Yo Ma. Like Condi, Yo-Yo Ma had a musical upbringing. His mother was a singer, and his father was a conductor and composer. At the age of eight Yo-Yo Ma appeared on American television in a concert conducted by Leonard Bernstein and would end up performing with most of the world's major orchestras. He attended Juilliard, then went to Harvard University.

Yo-Yo Ma met Condi when she was a dean at Stanford University and was teaching political science. At a reception dinner she approached him and told him that she played the piano. It was something he heard often from people who were introduced to him, so he wasn't overly impressed. But as the two continued to talk, he noticed that Condi knew what she was talking about. When he was notified that he was selected as an honoree at the National Humanities Awards at Constitution Hall and was asked whether he would like to perform, he called Condi to see if they could perhaps do a duet. She was honored.

Condi and Yo-Yo Ma got together the day before the event to practice, and during the awards program Condi accompanied Yo-Yo Ma on the piano, playing a graceful movement from Brahms's *Violin Sonata in D Minor* for an audience of two thousand. The duet by the cellist and pianist received a standing ovation after the performance.

In the summer of 2002 Condi was asked to speak at Stanford's commencement ceremonies. Reaching into her childhood memories that had been brutally brought back to the surface during 9/11, Condi told the twenty-four thousand people who gathered to hear her speak that the way to combat terrorism and hatred around the globe is through education. "Education is . . . the fundamental method of social progress and reform," she told the group, referring to the words of American philosopher John Dewey. In contrast, she said, terrorism seeks to "dehumanize and divide" people and society.

"Today, you are stepping into a world that is quite different than the one that existed when you arrived," she said. "It is a world that is more sober and sadder—clearer about its vulnerabilities—yet stronger, more conscious of our differences and yet more aware of our common humanity."[14]

Although it was a great moment for the graduates and their friends and family, the event had a sense of sobriety to it. As she talked about 9/11 and the terror that unfolded that fall day the year before, the guests' eyes glistened with tears. The wound was still fresh and would take many years to heal.

Condi continued to be the face and voice of the White House's defense against terror and seemed to be continually in the media soothing the wounds of the American people, defending the Bush Administration, and advocating for change. Still, she made time to spend with family and friends when the opportunity arose.

On New Year's Eve, with the promise of a new year before her, Condi and some friends flew to Jacksonville, Florida to watch Notre Dame play in the Gator Bowl at Alltel Stadium. After having dinner together they all met in Condi's hotel room, where they prayed for one another and the world and sang the hymn "His Eye Is on the Sparrow."

THE SECRETARY OF STATE YEARS

On March 20, 2003, the United States invaded Iraq. Termed Operation Iraqi Freedom by the military, the invasion marked the beginning of what is now called the Iraq War. While there was much controversy among our country's leaders about whether going to war was necessary, Condi became possibly the most outspoken supporter of it. As a result, as the death toll increased in the following months and years, she'd receive heavy criticism.

Senior Republicans approached Condi at the beginning of that year about running for the Senate in 2004, but she politely turned them down, saying that she had no desire to run for office. Later in the year it was rumored that she would run for governor of California against former actor and current governor Arnold Schwarzenegger in 2006. But when asked about it, her aides said she had no interest in being governor of California.

That spring Condi was asked by her cousin Anitra German if she'd be the commencement speaker at her graduation at the Mississippi College School of Law, and she agreed to do so. She told the packed room of graduates, friends, and family members that the values of freedom are not America's gift to the world but God's gift to humanity and that America would do whatever it takes to retain that liberation.

"People everywhere share the most basic yearning for liberty to create, speak and worship in freedom," she said. "When these values are under attack, we must not and we will not spare any effort in their defense."

Condi's passion for democracy at all costs was instilled in her from birth and was an enormous part of her heritage. The idea of some that it is sometimes better to let people live in the confines of bondage or that some would choose to live under Communist rule is absurd to her.

"I've watched over the last year and a half how people want to have human dignity worldwide. . . . We forget that when people are given a choice between freedom and tyranny, they will choose freedom. I remember all the stories before the liberation of Afghanistan that they wouldn't 'get it,' that they were all warlords and it would just be chaos. Then we got pictures of people dancing on the streets of Kabul just because they could listen to music or send their girls to school."

Condi fights for those who are afraid to do so for themselves. When other leaders are tired and want to just forget about moving forward because it's too hard, she stands up and insists they move forward. In many ways she is the voice of the underdog.

On June 23, 2003, in perhaps the most important affirmative action decision in thirty-five years, the Supreme Court upheld the University of Michigan Law School's policy, ruling that race can be one of the many factors considered by colleges when selecting their students because it furthers "a compelling interest in obtaining the educational benefits that flow from a diverse student body."

Condi continued to do her job and consciously made time to spend with her friends and family.

The following spring Condi was asked by the 9/11 Commission to testify under oath about the events that led to that tragedy and about the possibility that the National Security Counsel had ignored warnings that a terrorist attack was going to occur. Originally Condi refused to do so. President Bush claimed executive privilege under constitutional separation of powers and cited past traditions in refusing requests for her public testimony.

Under pressure, President Bush eventually agreed to allow her to publicly testify as long as it did not create a precedent of presidential staff being required to appear before the United States Congress whenever so requested. When all was said and done, her appearance before the commission on April 8, 2004 was deemed acceptable in part because she was not actually appearing before Congress. She thus became the first sitting National Security Advisor to testify on matters of policy.

For the second time President George W. Bush ran for office. During his campaign Condi became the first National Security Advisor to campaign for an incumbent president.

Condi used her position on the campaign as a soapbox to express her belief that Saddam Hussein's government in Iraq contributed to circumstances that produced terrorism like that of the 9/11 attacks on America, further supporting the President's decision to go to war.

President George Bush won the election and then nominated Condi for the role of Secretary of State, replacing her longtime friend Colin Powell. Condi and Powell considered one another as family. Powell's wife Alma also grew up in Birmingham and was very close to Condi. As a result of their bond, Condi often joined the Powells for dinner in their home. As a matter of fact, she ate there so frequently that when he'd bring Condi to their house after work he'd tell his wife, "Alma, Condi's home!"[1]

Upon her acceptance of the position on January 26, she became the nation's top diplomat as the country's sixty-sixth Secretary of State, at which point she became fourth in line to succeed the President in the event that he should die during his term. In doing so, she had a higher ranking in the presidential line of succession than any other woman has ever achieved (because Madeleine Albright is a naturalized U.S. citizen, she was ineligible to become President during her tenure as Secretary of State).

From the White House Roosevelt Room, President Bush sang Condi's praises. "During the last four years I have relied on her counsel, benefited from her great experience and appreciated her sound and steady judgment. . . . The Secretary of State is America's face to the world and in Dr. Rice the world will see the strength, the grace and the decency of our country."[2]

In 2004 there were accusations of racially motivated attacks upon Condi by three editorial cartoonists through the *Washington Post* and *New York Times*. Jeff Danzinger, Pat Oliphant, and Garry Trudeau used racial stereotypes to "conduct a personal character assassination of [Condi's] integrity because she has made the choice to serve in the Bush Administration," said Oliver Kellman, Jr., executive director of The Faith Based Leadership Council. "Dr. Rice has been singled out for persecution by a handful of bigoted liberals who have characterized her as a stepping and fetchin' sambo," Kellman further said. "I believe that they feel threatened and disturbed by the fact that Dr. Rice will soon be the most powerful Black woman in the United States as Secretary of State."[3]

Kellman was angry that the NAACP did not make a statement, intervene, or demand that the cartoonists issue an apology. Condi had no comment on the issue, and the issue seemed to have gone by the wayside. The silent overtone seemed to be that one must pick one's battles to win the war.

In February 2005 Condi went on an eight-day trip to Europe and the Middle East. Her purpose on this trip was to give the United States a fresh new image that would soothe the anger and frustration that other countries were expressing in regard to the Iraq War—and it worked beautifully. Newspapers across Europe sang Condi's praises.

After her meetings with dignitaries across Europe, Condi visited a Parisian music school, Conservatoire Hector Berlioz, where she listened to young protégés learn to play music. When given the opportunity to speak to the children, her advice for them was, "You have to practice and practice and practice."[4] She also shared that she was working to master a piano piece by Anton Dvorak.

As Condi filled the rather large shoes of her mentor and friend Colin Powell as Secretary of State, black advocates around the world gave a standing ovation. It wasn't necessarily her opinion on government issues and policies that gave her such praise, but the fact that she continues to push through the upper echelons of predominantly white males to make a name for herself—and for other black women. She was and would continue to be a role model not only for women generally but for black women in particular.

Representative Tom Lantos, a Democrat from California, and his wife Annette have been friends with Condi for years. So when they told Condi that their granddaughter, twenty-year-old singer Charity Sunshine, had been diagnosed with pulmonary hypertension, Condi's heart was moved to tears, and she suggested they do a fund-raiser to bring awareness and help educate people on the often-fatal disease that affects more than one hundred thousand people.

The Pulmonary Hypertension Association jumped on board and presented the concert on June 12, 2005. The event, dubbed "An Evening of Music, Friendship and Awareness," was hosted by Representative Lantos.

Sunshine met Condi at her condo the day before the concert so they could practice together, and as later told by Sunshine, "The piano bench is the most worn seat in the home." Similar to Condi, Sunshine was not new at performing in front of crowds. She had performed with orchestras around the world prior to this encounter with Condi.

The following evening at the Kennedy Center concert stage Condi accompanied Sunshine on several songs, including selections by Verdi, Mozart, and Jerome Kern. Eileen Cornett, director of a Master's degree program, opera coach, and solo and orchestral pianist at the Peabody Conservatory in Baltimore, accompanied Sunshine on a half-dozen other pieces. The unpublicized appearance was sold out and was a complete success.

On June 21, 2005 eighty-year-old Edgar Ray Killen, a one-time pastor and segregationist, was found guilty of manslaughter by a Mississippi jury for the 1964 murder of three young civil rights workers—a twenty-one-year-old black Mississippian, James Chaney, and two white New Yorkers, Andrew Goodman, twenty, and Michael Schwerner, twenty-four.

The youths had been working to register black voters during Freedom Summer and had gone to investigate the burning of a black church. They were falsely arrested by the Neshoba County Police on trumped-up charges in a conspiracy between the law enforcement agency and the Ku Klux Klan. The victims were imprisoned for several hours until it was dark, then released to the Ku Klux Klan, who beat and murdered them.

State prosecutors refused to try the case, claiming a lack of evidence. The federal government then stepped in, and the FBI arrested eighteen in connection with the killings in October 1964. In 1967 seven men were convicted on federal conspiracy charges and given sentences of three to ten years, but none served more than six, and none were tried on the charge of murder.

Federal judge William Cox, in defense of his lack of justice, and to the horror of many blacks and their sympathizers, said, "They killed one nigger, one Jew, and a white man. I gave them all what I thought they deserved." Another eight defendants were acquitted by their all-white juries, and another three ended in mistrials. One of those mistrials freed Edgar Ray Killen, believed to be the ringleader of the murderers. His case went to mistrial because the jury was deadlocked by one member who said she couldn't bear to convict a pastor. Killen was later retried and sentenced on the forty-first anniversary of the youths' murders.

Less than two months later, in late August, Hurricane Katrina hit, causing devastation along much of the north-central Gulf Coast of the United States. The costliest and one of the deadliest hurricanes in the history of the United States, Katrina all but completely consumed the city of New Orleans. At least 1,836 people lost their lives in Hurricane Katrina and in the subsequent floods in various other states, making it the deadliest U.S. hurricane since the 1928 Okeechobee Hurricane. In early September Condi toured her home state of Alabama for several days to view the damage it had received from Katrina.

On October 24, 2005 civil rights activist Rosa Parks died at the age of ninety-two. Parks had been diagnosed with progressive dementia the previous year. City officials in Montgomery and Detroit announced three days later that the front seats of their city buses would be reserved with black ribbons in honor of Parks until her funeral.

Condi attended Parks's memorial service on October 30 and stated that she and others who grew up in Alabama during the pinnacle of Parks's activism may not have realized her impact on her life at that time. "But I can honestly say that without Mrs. Parks, I probably would not be standing here today as Secretary of State."

That evening the casket was transported to Washington, D.C. and taken aboard a bus similar to the one in which Parks made her protest, to lay in honor in the U.S. Capitol Rotunda (making her the first woman and second African-American ever to receive this honor—the first was Officer Jacob Chestnut of the U.S. Capitol Police, who was gunned down in the Capitol in 1998). Her funeral followed on November 2.

Marriage, Babies, and the Presidency

*W*hen Condoleezza was nine years old, her parents took her to the White House. Standing outside the gate looking in, the youngster prophetically told her parents that one day she was going to be inside looking out instead of being on the outside looking in—and they believed her. They told her that when she grew up she could be anything, including President of the United States. The question America wants to know is, did she take her parents' words literally? The answer is both yes and no.

Condi obviously took her parents' words to heart—she has become everything she's wanted to be, which has included a wide range of high-profile positions. At fifty-two years of age she has far exceeded any and all expectations anyone has ever had for her. Since she's proven that she is capable, many have assumed that she will run for President. For the last two years almost every commentator who has interviewed Condi has asked her whether she plans to try for the Presidency in 2008. When she has emphatically answered, "No," they found other ways to ask the same question. When Tim Russert on NBC's *Meet the Press* interviewed Condi on the subject, her answers revealed her frustration over the often badgering question. "I've never wanted to run for anything, and I just don't have any desire to do it," she said.

"Desire or intention?" Russert said, provoking an answer.

"Both," she said. "Tim, I don't want to run for President."

"I will not run?" countered Russert.

Russert and Condi continued to play verbal Ping-Pong on the subject until Condi became obviously frustrated and said, "I will not run for President of the United States. How is that? I don't know how many ways to say 'no' in this town."

It still wasn't clear enough for those in Washington. It is as if they want to make sure her fingers were not crossed and want to hear her recite the childish chorus, "I tell the truth, I do not lie, I cross my heart and hope to die." They ask again and again, and she repeatedly gives the same answer.

"I never wanted to run for anything," Condi says. "I don't think I ran for class president at any time. . . . Look, I know what it takes to run for president. I've watched it up close a couple of times. I have enormous respect for people who will do that. But I want to do what I'm doing. I love being Secretary of State. . . . I liked being National Security Advisor. And one of these days very soon I'm going to want to return and be an academic again and get back to the California life and to the world of ideas."[1]

Condoleezza Rice is a woman of her word. There are times when she is vague, and there are times when she is direct. For example, she refers to herself as an "all-over-the-map Republican." She says she is "very conservative" in foreign policy, "ultra-conservative" in other areas, "almost shockingly libertarian" on some issues, "moderate" on others, and "liberal" on probably nothing.[2]

This statement is evasive, never really pinpointing what exactly she is conservative or liberal on apart from foreign policy. As a matter of fact, she has said that she plans on leaving the White House without anyone ever really knowing where she stands on specific issues—and such is the case thus far. But when she says no, she means no. If she was even remotely considering running for

President and she didn't want to reveal that as of yet, she'd say yes or nothing at all.

Unlike many politicians, Condi doesn't mince words and toss them out to media hounds before considering their impact on herself or others. She doesn't take back words that she said yesterday, last week, or even a year ago. Before she speaks she has rehearsed and packaged her words so precisely that she gives no room to question the motive or meaning behind them. As a matter of fact, she often uses the same speeches at various places, interchanging stories and facts to emphasize her point. But overall, her no means no, and her yes means yes, displaying a characteristic integrity that is often hard to find these days.

Former White House spokesman Scott McClellan was asked when he thought the United States would have its first woman President. In his answer he went on to speak about Condi as though it was a done deal. He noted that she had just returned from Liberia's inauguration of their first woman president, then caught himself and said, "But I'll avoid going there because I think she's made her views clear. But I have my personal thoughts about what a great job she would do."

On a separate occasion First Lady Laura Bush told CNN International that she believes the United States would probably have a woman President in one of the next few presidential elections and even said that she would "love" to see Condi run for the office. Then, just as McClellan did, she added, "She says she's definitely not running." On *Larry King Live* she added, "She'd make an excellent President, but I don't think we can talk her into running. . . . She sincerely does not want to run . . . [she] wants to move back to California and have a wonderful life teaching."[3]

Condi has never made decisions from an emotionally heightened place. The fact that she's capable of doing the job, that millions of people would like to see her do it, that it would continue to break numerous records for women and blacks, doesn't and will not sway or pressure her to run. Further, she's had multiple opportunities to climb the political ladder of success to the seat of the presidency and declined them all with the same adamant no.

So what will the all-star do? First and foremost, she tells family and friends, she'll move back "home" to Palo Alto, California. She desires to visit with family members whom she has not been able to see regularly.

"Sometimes I read [that] I have no family," says Condi. "I have [some] in the South, particularly in African-American families . . . extended family is really important. And I have aunts and uncles who are really, really close to me and marvelous friends . . . who go back to every stage in my life. . . . It's terrific."

Additionally Condi has said repeatedly that she wants to teach again at Stanford. Jackie Glaster, former director of the Boys and Girls Club of the Peninsula in Palo Alto, says that Condi also wants to again get involved with the youth program The Center for a New Generation, which she founded with her father in 1992.

"Condi has said that she is planning to come back to The Center for a New Generation," Glaster recently said. "She's not been able to support the program because of her appointment, but she's continued to give financially. Knowing her, I'm sure she is praying and looking to God for guidance and direction, and that gives me a certain sense of peace to know that's where her heart is and where her head is also."

Condi's family and closest friends echo Glaster's words. Repeatedly she has said she's going home and back to Stanford where she'll be welcomed, no doubt, with open arms. There is, however, one job she'd take out of state if offered to her—on Park Avenue in New York City—commissioner of the National Football League.

"I would love to work in sports management. One of the great moments in my job at Stanford was that I got to hire a football coach who took us to the Rose Bowl. That may be my highest achievement at Stanford," Condi said.[4]

She told Mike Freeman of the *New York Times*, "I think it

would be a very interesting job because I actually think football, with all due respect to baseball, is a kind of national pastime that brings people together across social lines, across racial lines. And I think it's an important American institution."

Interestingly enough, one aspect of Condi's passion for football is rooted in her study of the history of warfare. Condi has said that she's attracted to two fundamental similarities between football and warfare—the use of strategy and the goal of taking territory.

"I really consider myself a student of the game," Condi has said. "I find the strategy and tactics absolutely fascinating. I find the evolution of the game really interesting. Again, as it relates to military history. Military history has swung back and forth between advantage to the offense and advantage to the defense. When the offense has the advantage, then a new technology will come along that will temporarily give the defense the advantage and vice versa. Football has that kind of pattern, too."[5]

Not so different from her previous role of National Security Advisor, Condi prefers to focus on the tactics of the offense rather than the defense and also enjoys the ground game where there is physical contact, not unlike hand-to-hand combat.

Even while serving as National Security Advisor and Secretary of State, Condi has found a way to catch glimpses of games on television. And when that wasn't possible, she'd tape games—even after knowing who had won and who had lost—so she could watch them when she had time. She has often jokingly noted that she could have written several more books if she hadn't watched so many games on Sundays.

As far as her social life, friends say she was able to squeeze in a date or two during her tenure as the National Security Advisor and the Secretary of State. However, the time and availability of single, educated, and financially stable black men has been scarce at the top of the Hill.

"We talk about being married because both of us are single still," says Lori White. "But it is very difficult to be an African-

American woman with too much education. It isn't that we're not open to dating men who aren't African-American, but the choices that we have available to us are very different than for women who are not African-American.

"First of all, there is just the sheer numbers. The number of available men once you take out the men who might be in prison or who might not be available for whatever reason . . . that shrinks the pool. Then there are men who unfortunately are intimidated by those of us who have college degrees, and Condi and I both have Ph.D.s. Then there's the money factor. And based on what the Lord has allowed us to do career-wise, it's likely that we're also going to make more money than a lot of men with whom we might interact. You stack all that up, and it makes it very, very challenging.

"Then you have somebody like Condi who is Secretary of State," White says, laughing. "How does a guy ask her for a date? And if he does, there's no guarantee that if they make a date for Friday night she's going to be able to keep it. So we often talk about all of the challenges and difficulties."

But there's another reason Condi hasn't felt rushed to get married like so many other women—because the biological clock that ticks within her never made much of a sound to her ears.

"She was never interested in having children," says White. "Part of the reason for getting married is companionship, and the other part is to have a family. If you take away the family piece of it, then perhaps it's not as urgent to get married."

Another of Condi's close friends, Susan Ford, echoes White's words. "She [has] said she could imagine being married maybe at a later point in her life, but she never really wanted to have kids."

White says that Condi's life has been so consuming over the years that she's had to make sacrifices to do that which God has called her to do. If Condi had ever had children, she would have wanted to give them all the time and love that her parents gave her, which would have been impossible with her demanding career.

But Condi says it differently. In an interview for *The Washington*

Post when asked if she ever felt "obligated to continue the [Rice] bloodline," she said, "You mean, did I ever want kids? No. I think maybe it's because I'm an only child. I like children, but especially when they're 18." The next day she called the paper to elaborate. "I didn't start out not to get married and have children. . . . I don't regret that I couldn't pass on some of my genes, which sounds so incredibly narcissistic, but that I couldn't pass on some of the opportunities."[6]

White adds, "When Condi is done doing what she's doing and her life is a little bit more normal, then she will have more opportunity to pursue a normal relationship with someone. But the way her life is now, there's just no way. Even though the word on the street is that women can have it all, you can't—or you can't and do it right. To have both a career and to try to raise children well is very challenging to do. I don't know that Condi would have been able to become Secretary of State and have kids. There are sacrifices on one end or the other. There are sacrifices that women have to make that men don't have to make in the same way. Condi was never willing to settle for the wrong man just to have a family or to be in a relationship."

White goes on to say that Condi had a chance to be married and have children when she was engaged to Denver Broncos football player Rick Upchurch. "She was engaged in her early twenties when she was a student at Denver University, and she realized that he wasn't the right guy and it wasn't the right time. She's had her share of relationships over the course of time, but never anybody that she wanted to marry."

Condi agrees. "I am a very deeply religious person, and I have assumed that if I'm meant to get married God is going to somebody I can live with. And right now I haven't ever met anybody that I thought I could live with."

Condi also says that life never really unfolded for her to marry and have children. "Lives simply evolve," she says. "I didn't say, 'Oh, I think I'll have a career and not a family.' I don't think that's the way life happens. I really assume my life is working out the way it should, and I'm very happy in it. We're all individuals, and what is fulfilling is not the same for all of us. I'm so blessed in my life that I cannot imagine having an argument with God about whether my life should have turned out somehow differently. I can't even conceive of it."[7]

In fact, Condi does feel as though she has children—125 of them at The Center for a New Generation in Palo Alto, California, which she and her father founded together fifteen years ago, and she will no doubt invest time and money to keep the program running for years to come.

In regard to the rest of her future, Condi is not overly concerned. "I figure out a plan of action, and then I give it to God. . . . God's never failed me yet."[8]

Additionally she says she will follow her interests. "I've always felt that I've gotten where I am because I follow what interests me instead of worrying about the job market or what I ought to do. I'm also a very religious person and believe it's God's will to do certain things. You can't be rigid about your life. You can't have it all planned out far ahead of time."[9]

Not so ironically, Condi is not the only one from her era who has reaped success. Amazingly, the majority of the children who were raised in the same middle-class, black area of segregated Birmingham excelled in life. They not only rose above the prejudiced judgment that they were ignorant, worthless, and inferior, but they succeeded far beyond many of the whites who tried to beat them down. They became presidents of universities, college professors and administrators, politicians and doctors, lawyers and pastors. Most went to college. There is such a high success rate that a friend of Condi is considering writing a book about their successes.

Condi says that she is looking forward to leaving behind the all-consuming life she's experienced in the White House. She wants life to get back to normal as soon as possible. Her friends joke with her that she probably won't remember how to drive since she's been chauffeured around for seven years, but it's the day-to-day things like driving or going to a coffee shop or picking up clothes at the dry cleaner's that she misses the most.

After Condi moves back to Palo Alto, she'll likely attend Menlo Park Presbyterian Church again. She says that she enjoyed it there. Until then she will live at the Watergate Apartments where many other famous people in presidential administrations have lived before her. Additionally she will continue the things she's done since her arrival at the White House—go to concerts at the Kennedy Center, watch football, spend free moments with friends and family, play her grand piano, shop, and continue to attend church at the National Presbyterian Church in Washington, D.C.

As Condi herself shares: "I'm one of God's worst planners. I am actually not very good at having a plan for my life. When my students [came] to me the conversation usually [went] like this: 'Professor Rice, I'd like to talk to you about my future. How do I get to do what you do?' Usually this means, 'How do I get to work in the White House?' I have to tell them that you have to start out as a failed piano major which is what I did. You have to wander around until you find a subject that you're passionate about which for me was the Soviet Union, and then you have to stand back and have a lot of tolerance for ambiguity, for uncertainty, and for life taking twists and turns. It's an understatement to say that this isn't exactly the message that they're waiting to hear because they're looking for a plan for life.

"I've also not been particularly good at planning my personal life. I have a lot of friends, particularly women friends, who are currently planning to find a way to get married. And I'm not very good at that either and suspect that it might not work very well. So planning and life have never gone together particularly well for me, and it's served me generally pretty well not to plan.

"But in the last year or so, I have been struggling with the fact that I think I do need a plan for the development of my spiritual life, that that's one I can't leave to chance. And I've been struggling with

what the core of that plan ought to be, and I believe that the core
has to be understanding better, drawing better on the relationship
between faith, reason, and my everyday life. I think that there are
really three aspects to this plan for me, and I hope that in sharing
them with you, you may see some echoes of it that will be helpful in
your own plan for spiritual development.

"The first is, I have to have a better unity of faith and reason in
my personal life, in my personal relationship with God. Second, I
need to understand better and draw better on the role of my faith-
based community and friends in drawing faith and reason together.
And third, I need to understand better how God wants me to profess
my faith, proclaim my faith so that I might bring others to the unity
of faith and reason.

"Now, in some ways, I'm most comfortable with my personal
relationship with God. In fact, there's so much confirmation of
Christ in my life that faith and reason don't conflict in very important ways. I have been religious all my life. I cannot remember when
I did not believe. In fact, I was telling a friend the other day when
she said her daughter had chicken pox that I knew that chicken pox
was serious when I had it at six because it was the first time I got
to miss church.

"Church and God and Christianity were like breathing in my
family, so I was never one of those kids all the way through college
and through my adult life who doubted the existence of God. I cannot remember a single day when I did. My danger was quite another,
and that is that if you are that certain in your religious faith, you go
on autopilot about it, it just becomes like putting on a sweater in the
morning or eating breakfast in the morning. There's nothing very
special about the fact that you're religious. I, in fact, have sometimes
wished I had been one of those people with a conversion experience
when I was older and more competent to understand it because the
danger to just 'let it ride,' if you will, not growing in your personal
faith if you are as religious as I am, is very great.

"Some time ago, [my pastor] gave a sermon in which he talked about the prodigal son, and he had a particular bent on it that I found really helpful in this regard. And that was that this was really not a parable about how awful it was that this kid came back after having caroused for all those years and was accepted by his father while his older brother who'd been there toiling the fields for all of those years got jealous of this relationship with his newly-arrived-home brother. But rather this was about God really saying in many ways that there is a part of both of [them] in all of us; the one who goes off, but also the one who stays home and gets complacent. I saw so much of the one who stays home and gets complacent in myself that I decided that I really had to start trying to push the frontiers of my personal relationship with God. And for me, one of the impediments of this is my brain.

"Now I believe that God gave us [a brain] and he expects us to use it, but you must understand and you must feel that your intellect and your brain and your tendency to want to think everything through very often gets in the way of your faith. It seems to me that the faith of our fathers was somehow simpler than our faith, which is very complicated and complex and has to think everything through. So I've been dividing my questions about faith into several categories and asking myself, 'How comfortable am I in my head and in my faith and in the relationship between them?' Grace and faithfulness are not particularly hard concepts for me to either understand or believe because when I look at my own life, I see so many ways in which God has intervened and in which Christ has intervened that there isn't any conflict there. Redemption, eternal life, atonement, that's harder because in my brain I can't figure out what it means. I know that I'm really glad that I believe in eternal life. I know that has to be one of the things that attracts me to, that keeps me in this faith . . . the promise of eternal life. But is it just that I don't want to die? Is it just that I'm really glad that I don't think this is all there is? Or is it really an acceptance of eternal life and a belief that when I die, I'm going to be reunited with my Savior in a way that I could not possibly understand in my head?

"Eternal life, when you understand it in your head, is great because you can have all kinds of visions of what heaven is like and meeting those that you have not seen since they died and thank God you're not going to be submitted to the ground and never seen again. I mean, you understand why for those of us who are intellectuals and have read the great literature on this and heard the great music of it, this is something that's comforting. But when I ask, 'Have I made that bridge to really believing that I'm going to be one with God,' I'm not so sure. Another part of my personal development that needs work is letting go. For those of us who are accomplished, in one way or another we have been accomplished because we control the circumstances around us, not because the circumstances around us control us. When you think about it, that's how you become accomplished. You learn to figure out the cues, you learn to take the cues and push them in your own direction, you learn how to gain the system, you learn if you need to how to manipulate circumstances around you so that you get better. Well, it takes a lot of faith to step back from that rational, calculating approach and let go.

"Now, the second part of this plan is try to get closer to my church and my faith-based community. I was struck by my answers to a recent survey that [my church] did among members asking, 'What is it you'd like to know more about? What is it you'd like us to have small groups . . . classes on?' And almost everything that I checked was in the historical and political section. I'd like to know more about early Christianity. I'd like to know more about the history . . . and the governance of the Presbyterian church. I'm reminded that my father, who as a minister and a theologian, always said that if you're not careful, this is the part that really gets in the way of faith because if you know too much about the early Christian church, you may wonder what in the world they were doing.

"When you think about some of the struggles [the apostle] Paul had with the early Christians to get them to stop the kind of pettiness that they were engaging in, you do wonder about this organization that we have called 'the church.' And I dare say, with all due respect to ministers . . . you struggle a lot because churches can sometimes be the pettiest of places, the most political of places, the most difficult places [and you] wonder if you really can find God there. So I say to myself, 'Why am I interested in these, this part of the church?' Maybe it really is just intellectual interest. Maybe it is a way for faith and reason to work together. Maybe for me it's that I'm a political scientist and of course I'm interested in governance whether it's in Russia or in my church. Maybe that's why that particular set of topics appeals to me. But I suspect that it's really more, that it's a kind of window on the collectivity that is the church, the collectivity of Christians and the role of that, the role of being with other people of faith in trying to reinforce my beliefs but also to push the frontiers of my belief. There are people in our church who are so much more advanced in their personal relationship with God, in their personal relationships with Jesus, who really believe that Jesus meets every one of them personally. People who are so much more advanced than I am that I need to be around them. I need to draw on them. I also need to practice what I do.

"You know, I'm a pianist and it would never occur to me to not practice the piano if I'm going to continue to be a musician. So practice is important, and the practice of one's faith, not just at home but in the church with other people, is an important thing.

"There's another part of this that is a little bit of a mystery to me, and it was best said by one of my friends' mother whom I've known since [my childhood] in Birmingham. She was a member of my father's church. I said to her, 'Did you go to church today?' And she said, 'Of course,' and I was a little taken aback at that. And she said, 'I just don't feel right if I don't go to church.' And that said it best. It's really not that I believe somehow that God is going to judge me if I don't show up every Sunday. But there's something about the practice of going there, of participating in the sacrament and the Word and the traditions and the music, that's important to practice on a regular basis. And with Presbyterians, it's only an hour.

"My stepmother is a Baptist. That's a commitment! They go to church for a long time every Sunday. But for me, it's an hour. And sometimes I get so mad at myself when somehow I can't spare that hour to practice with other Christians of my religious faith.

"The most difficult and third part of my plan is to figure out what the role in all of this is of profession and proselytizing or . . . being a contagious Christian and what does that mean. And this is hard for a lot of reasons because while it is safe in many ways to practice your personal faith, while it is safe to go into a community of believers, going out there and talking about being a believer is a much, much harder thing to bridge. And there, for me, faith and reason have really got to come together because while I might say to a group of believers, 'Well, I just believe' and that'll be accepted, it's much harder to say that to people who don't believe.

"I was really struck by the comment of a friend who read an article about me in the *San Jose Mercury News*. In this article it said that I was an evangelical Christian. This very good friend of mine said, 'You know, that was a great article about you . . . but you're not an evangelical Christian.' And I thought, 'Yeah, but I am.' But I started wondering what was it about me that those words somehow in her mind didn't fit who I was. She knows I'm a Christian. Now, I think part of it may be, quite frankly, that we as evangelicals are increasingly speaking in language and in ways that simply turns people off and when they meet one of us that they like, they can't possibly believe that we're actually evangelical.

"I worry a lot about the government and the church. I worry a lot about trying to legislate morality. A friend of mine said, 'You can't legislate love. You can't legislate values.' I worry a lot that what we have done is to sound judgmental and exclusive in the way that we talk to people about the role of our faith in what we do. Whatever the issue . . . this tendency to speak in such loud and judgmental tones has really hurt the message that we're trying to deliver. In fact, what's very interesting to me is that if you think about the way that Christ tried to meet those who did not believe, it was quite opposite. He didn't shout at them. He tried to meet them where they were. And he met every person in a different place with a different way of dealing with it. For the young ruler, he was pretty tough: 'You have no chance to get into the Kingdom of Heaven essentially if you don't change your ways.' With the woman at the well, it was a much softer approach because of the deepness of her hurt. In the healing ministries, it was showing what faith could be . . . my favorite hymn is 'Dear Lord and Father of Mankind,' and it says, 'Speak through the earthquake, wind and fire, O still, small voice of calm.' And so shouting at people and judging them and browbeating them can't be the right way to open up the possibilities of faith to them. So I ask myself, 'What is?'

"In part, [speaking like this] is part of professing faith. But I'll tell you, I'm more comfortable giving a speech about faith than I am when I'm one-on-one with somebody trying to talk about faith and trying to open up that possibility to them, finding that I have to use faith and reason together in order to do it . . . it's actually not hard to get people to the practical lessons that Christ taught about love and about caring for one another. That's the sort of easy part of the theology because even nonbelievers are attracted to what Christ meant in terms of his sort of practical advice for how we should get along with each other. And I think drawing on that is absolutely important, but the fact is, nonbelievers can also be kind. Nonbelievers can also be people who treat others well. In fact, sometimes nonbelievers treat people better than believers do. And so we've got a little gap between faith and reason when we start thinking about how Christianity has played itself out over our history. But I think that the problem is if you only deal with Christ at the level of good works, and to be sure there are many good works. Let me just say as a student of international politics, what the church is doing and faithful people are doing in places like Russia and places like China and places like Nigeria is a miracle, and those good works need to be celebrated and understood. But if we only play on that plain, which really is the plain in which reason comes into being, I think that we're missing the more important part of our message.

"Now, the optimism that comes with faith is part of that message. An acceptance of good and bad times as all part of a larger plan is a part of that message. A certainty that you're held in God's hands gives you an ability to tolerate ambiguity, an ability to tolerate uncertainty, an ability to try and give up and believe, as I tell my students, that it's all going to work out as it should. You really shouldn't worry every day at nineteen about what you're going to do at fifty-five. It allows you to have a little bit of distance from day to day. But there is another part of this that is especially difficult, and that's what I call 'the complications of theology, the mysteries.' I went to Catholic high school, and I went to Notre Dame, and so I've been to Mass a lot. And there's a point at which they say in Mass, 'Let us proclaim the mysteries of our faith. Christ has died, Christ has risen, Christ will come again.' That's the mystery of faith. And that's the part that I find just incredibly difficult to bridge reason and faith in a way that I can talk about it to help others accept that mystery of faith. And so I think that I'm not a mature enough Christian just yet to have an answer; maybe I never will be. How do you help others come to the mystery of faith? But I know one thing, and that is that I have to do it quietly, I have to do it one-on-one, I have to be willing to talk about what faith means to me in a rational way; I have to be able to talk about what faith means to me day-to-day, I have to be able to talk about why I believe. But more importantly, I have to have an approach that stands back and realizes that maybe none of us are ever going to be mature enough to bridge that. That's God's work. It's only through really coming personally to accept Christ, personally to accept God, that one begins to believe in the deepest of one's soul that mystery of faith that Christ died, Christ has risen, and Christ will come again. And so in part of my plan, I intend to try to spend time with people who appear to be hungry for that message, but to also try to get them to engage with Christians who are more mature than I am and perhaps most importantly to try to get them to a place like the church where perhaps some of those mysteries that bridge faith and reason for those of us who are believers can begin to bridge faith and reason for them.

"I know that whatever is ahead for me, and I'm very excited about the next years—whatever comes next, the reason that I can be as excited as I am, really with very little trepidation, but as excited as I am, is that I really do believe that it was God's plan for me to be where I am today and that God has a plan for me to be someplace in the future. And part of my bridging faith and reason is going to be let him lead where I can follow in a way that I hope serves his purpose, not just my own.

". . . [God's] voice . . . can speak in the tumultuous times, a voice that can speak when everything's roaring around you. Clearly it has for my ancestors in slavery and for Jews in the Holocaust and for the most tumultuous times. I think that our challenge, my challenge, is to be quiet enough not just to go through what I call prayers of petition, you know? When you sit there and you pray the same prayer every night: 'Please take care of so-and-so.' 'Could you help me with that speech tomorrow?' . . . [Not just] being quiet for a while and not asking God what he can do for you, but letting God speak to you about what it is he needs you to do for yourself and how he's going to be a part of that, and so that's one of the parts of the still, small voice for me. The other piece is how we approach others because I think that we have to realize that this is a pretty incredible message, and I mean that in the true sense of the word *incredible*—not a remarkable message, but for people who don't believe, those mysteries are just hard to grasp, hard to believe. And sometimes people look at you like you've sort of lost your mind. So I think that not getting into an argument about it is one way to think about the still, small voice. How can Christ get through in this conversation if you're just intent on making a point? Right? If you're just intent on saying, 'I know that Christ will come again, and I'm going to give you ten arguments as to why that is, and you're just kind of stupid that you don't get it' . . . Which is somehow the way that we argue, you know? We argue about faith in the way that we argue about anything else. And I think that's a little bit of the problem with reason and faith. So it's also when you approach others—for me, it has been more to listen than to talk, to gently prod more than push, recognizing that I'm not going to bridge the distance between the intellect and the mysteries. Christ is going to bridge the difference between mysteries and the intellect, and if I'm just talking real loud, He doesn't have room to do it."[10]

Conclusion

*W*hen I began the research necessary for this book, I had a certain expectation of what Condi's faith should look like if she were a *real* Christian. Specifically, her faith would fit into the box I'd created that contained my specific denominational beliefs, convictions, and passions. Isn't that what we as Christians tend to do? Unless other believers fit into our cookie-cutter molds of denomination we disregard them as inauthentic. But as I researched, interviewed, wrote, and in the true sense of the word experienced her life in much detail, I realized that the root of Condi's faith is the same as mine. Because our upbringings were different and our adult lives are on separate ends of the spectrum, our faith simply manifests itself in ways that are not the same. If you strip away our career choices, the drastic difference in schooling we received, and the pretensions that come with both, you will find two women with ultimately the same passion and goals—to live a life that is uninhibitedly surrendered to God, to share the joy of that life with others, to use the gifts given by God to impact the world, and to help lead others to the saving knowledge of Jesus Christ.

Condi loves the Lord. Her life is a reflection of that admiration. Friends who know her best and those in her inner circle who are not God-fearing Christians know her to reflect the characteristics and traits evident in the Bible and the life of Jesus—love, joy, peace, patience, kindness, goodness, faithfulness, gentleness, and self-control. That is not to say she's perfect, for none of us are. We all are sinners in need of a Savior, and Condi is no exception to that reality.

Like all of us, Condi has experienced heartaches, disappointments, and setbacks. She has worked hard to move beyond them, and her faith has been the steering rod that has driven her passion—not just for success, but for contentment. Like her forefathers, she has lived a life that has been orchestrated by God. Her parents, grandparents, great-grandparents, and those before them helped pave the way for Condi. She, in turn, is paving the way for others. It hasn't been just family members who have cut through the thicket and carved out a trail for her to walk down. Credit must be given to the many blacks and their sympathizers who fought for the freedom Condi relishes now, although the battle is not over yet. At the Republican National Convention in 2000 Condi told the nation, "Democracy in America is still a work in progress. But even with its flaws this unique American experience provides a shining beacon to people who still suffer in places where ethnic difference is a license to kill."

What is freedom anyway? Is it merely physical? I think not. Despite the confines of our environment and the captivity of our physical bodies from its effects, true liberation is found internally through the saving knowledge of Jesus Christ and an intimate relationship with him. It's something that laws or people can't take away from us. Condi's family knew that truth. Their recipe for freedom from the beginning started with their faith, extended to their family, and as a by-product fueled their passion for democracy in the world—and it succeeded.

Timeline and Key Facts About Condoleezza Rice

PERSONAL INFORMATION

Born in Birmingham, Alabama, November 14, 1954.

Languages: Russian, Spanish, English, French, with research ability in Czech and French.

Raised in the Presbyterian denomination.

EDUCATION

Ph.D., Graduate School of International Studies, University of Denver, 1981.

M.A., University of Notre Dame, 1975.

B.A., University of Denver, 1974—*cum laude* and Phi Beta Kappa.

TEACHING INTERESTS

International politics.

Politics of Europe, Central Europe, and the former Soviet Union.

International security policy.

COMPARATIVE STUDY OF MILITARY INSTITUTIONS.

PROFESSIONAL EXPERIENCE

Secretary of State, 2005–present.

National Security Advisor, 2000–2004.

Provost, Stanford University, September 1993–June 1999.

Professor of political science, Stanford University, May 1993–December 1994.

Special Assistant to the President for National Security Affairs and Senior Director for Soviet Affairs, National Security Council, March 1990–1991.

Director, Soviet and East European affairs, National Security Council, February 1989–March 1990.

Associate professor of political science, Stanford University, September 1987–April 1993.

Assistant professor of political science, Stanford University, 1981–1987.

Council on Foreign Relations, International Affairs Fellow (Special Assistant to the Director, Joint Chiefs of Staff), 1986–1987.

Assistant director, Center for International Security and Arms Control, Stanford University, 1981–1986.

American Association for the Advancement of Slavic Studies.

Intern, The Rand Corporation, 1980.

Intern, United States Department of State, Summer 1977.

FELLOWSHIPS AND HONORS

Fellow, American Academy of Arts and Sciences, 1997.

John P. McGovern Medal of Sigma Xi, The Scientific Research Society, 1996.

Honorary Doctorate, University of Notre Dame, 1995.

Doctor of Humane Letters (honorary degree), University of Alabama, 1994.

Humanities and Sciences Dean's Award for Distinguished Teaching, 1993.

Doctor of Laws (honorary degree), Morehouse College, 1991.

Hoover Institution for War and Peace Fellow (by courtesy), 1991–1993.

Institute for International Studies Senior Fellow, Stanford University, 1991–1994.

International Affairs Fellow, Council on Foreign Relations, 1986–1987.

National Fellow, Hoover Institution on War and Peace, 1985–1986.

Walter J. Gores Award for Excellence in Teaching (Stanford), 1984.

Delegate to the Bellagio "New Faces" Conference (Arms Control

Association and International Institute for Strategic Studies), 1984.

Arms Control Fellow, Stanford University, 1980–1981.

Ford Foundation Fellow, 1980–1981.

National Fund Fellowship for Outstanding Minority Graduate Students, 1977–1980.

Denver Social Science Foundation Fellow, 1976–1977.

University of Notre Dame First Year Graduate Fellow, 1974–1975.

Phi Beta Kappa, University of Denver, 1974.

University of Denver Honors Scholarship, 1971–1974.

BOARDS AND COMMITTEES

Board of Directors, William and Flora Hewlett Foundation, 1997–1999.

Board of Trustees, Notre Dame University, 1997–1999.

International Advisory Council, J.P. Morgan, 1995–1999.

Board of Trustees, Carnegie Corporation of New York, 1994–1997.

Board of Directors, The Rand Corporation, 1992–1997.

Board of Directors, Hewlett-Packard, 1991–1993.

Trustee, National Endowment for the Humanities, 1991–1993.

Board of Directors, Chevron Corporation, 1991–1999.

Board of Directors, Transamerica Corporation, 1991–1999.

Board of Directors, Carnegie Endowment for International Peace, 1989.

COMMUNITY SERVICE AND NATIONAL SERVICE

Federal Advisory Committee on Gender Integrated Training in the Military, 1997.

Vice president, Boys and Girls Club of the Peninsula, 1996–1999.

Founding board member, The Center for a New Generation, 1992–1999.

Member of Governor's Advisory Panel on Redistricting California, 1991.

Consultant, National Security Council, 1991–1993.

KQED Public Broadcasting Board of Directors, 1989.

Consultant, Joint Chiefs of Staff, 1986–1988.

Mid-Peninsula Urban Coalition Board of Directors, 1984–1985; 1987–1988.

PROFESSIONAL ACTIVITIES AND ASSOCIATIONS

Address to the Republican National Convention, August 1992.

American Political Science Association.

Aspen Strategy Group, 1991–1995.

Commonwealth Club Address, May 1988 and December 1991.

Consultant on Soviet Affairs, ABC News, 1991.

Council on Foreign Relations, lifetime member.

Lincoln Club of Northern California.

Speaker, SPASO House (U.S. Ambassador's Residence) Lecture Series, Moscow, April 1988.

UNIVERSITY ACTIVITIES

Provost's Committee on the Status of Women in the University, 1992–1994.

University Policy and Planning Board, 1992–1993.

Search Committee for the President of the University, 1991.

Search Committee for the Dean of Admissions, 1991.

Search Committee for Stanford football coach, 1988, 1991.

Department of Political Science: chair, Graduate Admissions Committee, 1991, 1992; Director of Graduate Studies, 1988–1989; Policy and Planning Committee, 1983–1984, 1987–1988.

National Centennial Campaign Faculty, 1988–1989.

Executive Committee, Institute for International Studies, 1988–1989, 1991–1993.

Faculty Senate, 1988–1989.

Public Service Center Steering Committee, 1987 and 1991–1999 (chair).

Presidential Committee for the Selection of the Vice President and Provost, 1983–1984.

Freshman advisor, 1982–1985.

Committee on Undergraduate Admissions and Financial Aid, 1982–1985; 1988–1989 (chair).

PUBLICATIONS

Books

Germany Unified and Europe Transformed: A Study in Statecraft, with Philip Zelikow (Cambridge, MA: Harvard University Press, 1995).

The Gorbachev Era, edited with Alexander Dallin (Palo Alto, CA: Stanford Alumni Press Service, 1986).

Uncertain Allegiance: The Soviet Union and the Czechoslovak Army (Princeton, NJ: Princeton University Press, 1984).

Articles

"The Military Under Democracy," *Journal of Democracy*, April 1992.

"Soviet Grand Strategy," in Paul Kennedy, ed., *Grand Strategy* (New Haven, CT: Yale University Press, 1991).

"The Soviet General Staff's View of War," in Michael Fry, ed., *History of the White House and the Kremlin* (London/New York: Pinter, 1991).

"A New Army for a New State," *Time Magazine,* September 3, 1991.

"The General Staff: Learning from the World War II Experience," in Jonathan R. Adelman and Christann Gibson, eds., *Contemporary Soviet Military Affairs* (Boston: Unwin Hyman, 1989).

"US-Soviet Relations and the Reagan Legacy," in Larry Berman, ed., *The Reagan Legacy* (Berkeley: University of California Press, 1989).

"Soviet Command and Control and Crisis Stability," with David Holloway, in Bruce Blair and Kurt Gottfried, eds., *Crisis Stability* (New York: Oxford University Press, 1988).

"SALT and the Search for a Security Regime," in Alexander George, Philip Farley, and Alexander Dallin, eds., *US-Soviet Security Cooperation, Achievements, Failures, Lessons* (New York: Oxford, 1988).

"Defense Decision-Making in the Soviet Union: Is Gorbachev Changing the Rules of the Game?" *Journal of International Affairs* (Spring 1988); updated version reprinted in Frederic J. Fleron, Jr., Erik P. Hoffman, Robbin F. Laird, *Contemporary Issues In Soviet Foreign Policy* (New York: Walter de Gruyter, 1991).

"The Party, the Military and Decision Authority in the Soviet Union," *World Politics* (October 1987).

"Gorbachev and the Military," *Current History* (September 1986).

"The Makers of Soviet Strategy," in Gordon Craig and Peter Paret, *The Makers of Modern Strategy* (Princeton, NJ: Princeton University Press, 1986).

"The Military-Technical Revolution and the General Staff in the Soviet Union," in Herbert Goodman, *Science and Technology in the Soviet Union* (Stanford Conference Report on Soviet Technology, 1984).

"Warsaw Pact Reliability: The Czechoslovak People's Army," in Daniel Nelson, ed., *The Problem of Reliability in the Warsaw Pact* (Boulder, CO: Westview Press 1984).

"Defense Burdensharing in the Warsaw Pact," in Jane M. O. Sharp and David Holloway, eds., *The Warsaw Pact* (New Haven, CT: Yale University Press, 1984).

"The Politics of Nuclear Weapons in the Warsaw Pact," in Jeffrey Boutwell, ed. *Theater Nuclear Forces in Europe* (Cambridge, MA: Ballinger, 1984).

"Political Terror in Czechoslovakia," in Jonathan Adelman, ed., *Terror in Communist Systems* (Boulder, CO: Westview Press, 1983).

"The Soviet Decision to Invade Hungary" (with Michael Fry), *Studies in Comparative Communism*, Winter 1983.

"The Czechoslovak People's Army," in Jonathan Adelman, ed., *Communist Armies in Politics* (Boulder, CO: Westview Press, 1982).

"The Problem of Elite Cohesion in the Warsaw Pact," *Air University Review,* April 1981.

NOTES

CHAPTER 1: A STORY OF PREJUDICE AND PROMISE
1. *Brown Et Al. v. Board of Education of Topeka Et Al.* Appeal from the United States District Court for the District of Kansas. No. 1.
2. "The Responsibilities and Opportunities of an Educated Person," Stanford University News Service, June 19, 2002, p. 2.
3. "Lessons of Might and Right," *Washington Post*, September 10, 2001.
4. Ibid.
5. Ibid.

CHAPTER 2: A LOVE STORY
1. "Condi: The Girl Who Cracked the Ice," *The Sunday Times*, November 21, 2004.
2. "The Responsibilities and Opportunities of an Educated Person," Stanford University News Service, June 19, 2002, p. 2.

CHAPTER 3: RAISED IN THE WAR ZONE
1. Leslie Montgomery, *Were It Not for Grace* (Nashville: Broadman & Holman, 2005), p. 6.
2. "A Lesson from Condoleezza Rice," http://www.racematters.org/lessonon lifecondoleezzarice.htm.
3. "Lessons of Might and Right," *The Washington Post*, September 9, 2001, p. W-23.
4. *Lansing State Journal*, Condoleezza Rice remarks to 2004 Michigan State University graduates.
5. "Condoleezza Rice: Balancing Act," *The Stanford Magazine*, Winter 1985, p. 19.
6. Stanford University News Service, May 2002 commencement ceremony.
7. *American Experience*, "The Murder of Emmett Till," People & Events, www.pbs.org/wgbh/amex/till/.
8. *Sweatt v. Painter*, 339 U.S. 629 (1950). Certiorari to the Supreme Court of Texas. No. 44.
9. *McLaurin v. Oklahoma State Regents*, 339, U.S. 637 (1950). Appeal from the United States District Court for the Western District of Oklahoma. No. 34
10. Montgomery, *Were It Not for Grace*, p. 9.
11. See http://www.joyfulheart.com/misc/Newton.htm.
12. Montgomery, *Were It Not for Grace*, p. 9.
13. "Lessons of Might and Right," *The Washington Post*, September 10, 2001.
14. "Condi: The Girl Who Cracked the Ice," *The Sunday Times*, November 21, 2004.
15. Civil Rights Museum, Birmingham, Alabama, Statistics, Archives.

16. "Soviets Face Hard Choices in Arms Control, Rice Says," Stanford University News Service, December 2, 1983.
17. "Condoleezza Rice: Balancing Act."

CHAPTER 4: THE ADOLESCENT YEARS

1. National Presbyterian Church, Washington, D.C., Testimony of Condoleezza Rice, *Washington Times*, August 27, 2002; also see http://chebar0.tripod.com/id117.htm.
2. Leslie Montgomery, *Were It Not for Grace* (Nashville: Broadman & Holman, 2005).
3. U.S. Department of State, Remarks with United Kingdom Foreign Secretary Jack Straw at the Blackburn Institute's Frank A. Nix Lecture, October 21, 2005, University of Alabama.
4. Birmingham Civil Rights Museum.
5. Diane McWhorter, *A Dream of Freedom, the Civil Rights Movement From 1954 to 1968* (New York: Scholastic, 2004), pp. 6-7.
6. Remarks with United Kingdom Foreign Secretary Jack Straw.
7. "Condoleezza Rice, Superstar," Stanford News Service.
8. Birmingham Civil Rights Museum, Archives.
9. See http://www.state.gov/secretary/rm/2005/55423.htm.
10. "Soviets Face Hard Choices in Arms Control, Rice Says" The Stanford News Service, December 2, 1983.
11. Ibid.
12. The Stanford University News Service, November 12, 1985.
13. "The Most Powerful Woman in the World," *Essence*, February 2002.
14. "The President's Prodigy," *Vogue*, October 2001.
15. Stanford University 2002 graduation ceremony.
16. "Condi: The Girl That Cracked the Ice," *The Sunday Times*, November 21, 2004.
17. "The Most Powerful Woman in the World."
18. University of Denver, Archives.
19. The White House Biographies, Whitehouse.gov., John Fitzgerald Kennedy. See http://www.britannica.com/eb/article-9116924/Document-John-F-Kennedy-The-American-Promise-to-African-Americans.

CHAPTER 5: THE PRE-TEEN YEARS

1. "The Most Powerful Woman in the World," *Essence*, February 2002.
2. "Lessons of Might and Right," *Washington Post*, September 10, 2001.
3. See www.Spartacus.schoolnet.co.uk/JFKrussell.htm.
4. "Condi: The Girl Who Cracked the Ice," *The Sunday Times*, November 21, 2004.
5. Ibid.

6. Leslie Montgomery, *Were It Not for Grace* (Nashville: Broadman & Holman, 2005), p. 8.

CHAPTER 6: THE TRANSFORMATION OF A WOMAN-CHILD
1. John Rice's personal notes, University of Denver, Archives.
2. "The Responsibilities and Opportunities of an Educated Person," Stanford University News Service, June 19, 2002, p. 1.
3. Thompson Gale, Women's History, Condoleezza Rice; www.galegroup. com/free_resources/whm/bio/rice_c.htm.
4. "The Top of Her Game," *Essence Magazine*, February 2002.
5. Leslie Montgomery, *Were It Not for Grace* (Nashville: Broadman & Holman, 2005), p. 9.
6. Ibid.
7. WNYC, "Mad About Music: Condoleezza Rice," January 2, 2005.
8. "Condoleezza Rice: Balancing Act," *The Stanford Magazine*, Winter 1985.
9. "Soviets Face Hard Choices in Arms Control, Rice Says," Stanford University News Service, December 2, 1983.

CHAPTER 7: THE DEVELOPMENT OF A SOVIET EXPERT
1. See http://gos.sbc.edu/r/rice.html. Gifts of Speech, Republican National Convention Remarks, August 1, 2000.
2. *Lansing State Journal*, Condoleezza Rice's remarks to 2004 Michigan State University graduates.
3. Ibid.
4. "Soviets Face Hard Choices in Arms Control, Rice Says," Stanford University News Service, December 2, 1983.
5. Ibid.
6. "The President's Prodigy," *Vogue*, October 2001.
7. "The Christian Testimony of Condoleezza Rice," *The Layman*, October 2002; www.layman.org.
8. National Presbyterian Church, Washington, D.C., Testimony of Condoleezza Rice, *Washington Times*, August 27, 2002; also see http://chebar0. tripod.com/id117.htm.

CHAPTER 8: THE STANFORD YEARS
1. "Condoleezza Rice: Balancing Act," *The Stanford Magazine*, Winter 1985.
2. Leslie Montgomery, *Were It Not for Grace* (Nashville: Broadman & Holman, 2005), p. 10.
3. Ibid.
4. Ibid.

CHAPTER 9: THE SCOWCROFT YEARS

1. "The President's Prodigy," *Vogue*, October 2001.
2. "Velvet-glove Forcefulness, Six Years of Provostial Challenges and Achievements," *Stanford Report*, June 9, 1999.
3. *The Clarion*, University of Denver newspaper, April 19, 1990, National Security Council's Director of Soviet Affairs.

CHAPTER 10: THE TURBULENT YEARS

1. "Casper Selects Condoleezza Rice to Be Next Stanford Provost," Stanford University News Service, May 19, 1993.
2. "Lessons of Might and Right," *The Washington Post*, April 28, 2004.
3. "The President's Prodigy," *Vogue*, October 2001.
4. "Casper Selects Condoleezza Rice to Be Next Stanford Provost."
5. Ibid.
6. Ibid.
7. Ibid.
8. Ibid.
9. "The Top of Her Game," *Essence*, February 2002.
10. "Casper Selects Condoleezza Rice."
11. Ibid.
12. "The Top of Her Game."
13. "Casper Selects Condoleezza Rice."
14. "Velvet-glove Forcefulness," *Stanford Report*, June 9, 1999.
15. Leslie Montgomery, *Were It Not for Grace* (Nashville: Broadman & Holman, 2005).

CHAPTER 11: A SEASON OF CHANGE AND LOSS

1. Steven Emerson, "The Other Fundamentalists," *New Republic*, June 12, 1995, p. 40.
2. Statements of Mohammed A. Salameh, Nidal Ayyad, Mahmud Abouhalima, and Amad Mohammad Ajaj at sentencing, *United States of America v. Muhammad A. Salameh et. al.*, S1293CR 180 (KTD), May 24, 1994, pp. 26-34, 41-49, 53-65, 65-113, Government Exhibit 196.
3. *Stanford Report*, December 9, 1998, p. 1.
4. "Rice to Step Down," Stanford University News Service, December 9, 1998, p. 1.
5. "Rice Steps Down to Pursue Her Passion," *The Stanford Magazine*, January/February 1999.
6. National Presbyterian Church, Washington, D.C., Testimony of Condoleezza Rice, *Washington Times*, August 27, 2002; also see http://chebar0.tripod.com/id117.htm.

7. Leslie Montgomery, *Were It Not for Grace* (Nashville: Broadman & Holman, 2005).

CHAPTER 12: FROM THE INSIDE LOOKING OUT
1. Leslie Montgomery, *Were It Not for Grace* (Nashville: Broadman & Holman, 2005).
2. *Oprah*, "Secrets of Women Who Rule," October 17, 2003, transcript, p. 12.
3. Ibid.
4. "The Most Powerful Woman in the World," *Essence*, February 2002.
5. Ibid.
6. National Presbyterian Church, Washington, D.C., Testimony of Condoleezza Rice, *Washington Times*, August 27, 2002; also see http://chebar0.tripod.com/id117.htm.
7. CNN, *Larry King Live*. See http://transcripts.cnn.com/TRANSCRIPTS/0505/11/lkl.01.html.
8. "Walk of Faith—Condoleezza Rice," *Washington Times*, August 27, 2002; see http://chebar0.tripod.com/id117.htm.
9. "Secrets of Women Who Rule," p. 12.
10. Montgomery, *Were It Not for Grace*.
11. "Walk of Faith—Condoleezza Rice."
12. "The Top of Her Game," *Essence*, February 2002.
13. "Rice Leads Counterattacks," CBS news, March 28, 2004; see www.cbsnews.com/stories/2004/03.28/60minutes/main609074.shtml.
14. "National Security Advisor . . . to Use Education to Counter Hatred," Stanford University News Service, June 19, 2002, p. 1.

CHAPTER 13: THE SECRETARY OF STATE YEARS
1. "The Most Powerful Woman in the World," *Essence*, February 2002.
2. White House Archives.
3. The Qando Blog, Free Markets, Free People, November 21, 2004; see www.qando.net/details.aspx?Entry=485.
4. "Love Her or Leave Her, Condi Rice Still Does Black Women Proud," February 9, 2005; see www.blackamericaweb.com/site.aspx/bawnews/condirice210.

CHAPTER 14: MARRIAGE, BABIES, AND THE PRESIDENCY
1. CBS's *Face the Nation*, March 13, 2005.
2. "Bush's Secret Weapon," March 20, 2000; see http://archive.salon.com/politics2000/feature/2000/03/20/rice/.
3. See www.whitehouse.gov/news/releases/2006/03/200603243.htm.
4. "On Pro Football; Dream Job for Rice: N.F.L. Commissioner," *The New York Times*, April 17, 2002.

5. See http://news.bbc.co.uk/2/hi/americas/4019395.stm.
6. "Lessons of Might and Right," *The Washington Post*, September 2001.
7. "The Top of Her Game," *Essence*, February 2002.
8. National Presbyterian Church, Washington, D.C., Testimony of Condoleezza Rice, *Washington Times*, August 27, 2002; also see http://chebar0.tripod.com/id117.htm.
9. "Condoleezza Rice: Balancing Act," *The Stanford Magazine*, Winter 1985.
10. Speaking engagement at Menlo Park Presbyterian Church in Palo Alto, California.

If you would like to contact the author, you can reach her in the following ways:

By Letter:
Leslie Montgomery
The Pool at Bethesda Ministries
P.O. Box 300
Lake Norden, South Dakota 57248

By e-mail:
princesswarrior@lesliemontgomery.com

Via the Internet:
www.lesliemontgomery.com

Are you looking for peace? Go to www.lesliemontgomery.com, and doubleclick on the "Looking for Peace" tab for information on how to obtain peace.